Summary of Contents

I0005483

LEVEL UP YOUR WEB APPS WITH GO

BY MAL CURTIS

Level Up Your Web Apps With Go

by Mal Curtis

Product Manager: Simon Mackie   **English Editor**: Kelly Steele

Technical Editor: Lionel Barrow   **Cover Designer**: Alex Walker

Published by SitePoint Pty. Ltd.

48 Cambridge Street Collingwood
VIC Australia 3066
Web: www.sitepoint.com
Email: business@sitepoint.com

ISBN 978-0-9924612-9-4 (print)

ISBN 978-0-9941826-0-9 (ebook)
Printed and bound in the United States of America

About Mal Curtis

Mal Curtis is a Kiwi polyglot software engineer currently focusing on Go and JavaScript. He's the founder of transactional email management service Apostle.io, and is a Principal Engineer at Vend, where he helps make beautiful Point of Sale and Inventory Management software (yes, it can be beautiful). In the past he's helped launch Learnable.com, and worked for SitePoint in Melbourne. In his spare time you'll find him attempting geeky pursuits with varying levels of failure, such as quadcopters and sous vide cooking.

About SitePoint

SitePoint specializes in publishing fun, practical, and easy-to-understand content for web professionals. Visit http://www.sitepoint.com/ to access our blogs, books, newsletters, articles, and community forums. You'll find a stack of information on JavaScript, PHP, Ruby, mobile development, design, and more.

To my Dad — for surrounding me with technology from my earliest days, I can never thank you enough. I miss you.

And to Sarah — for your unrelenting support and patience. You're my rock.

Table of Contents

Chapter 6   Gophr Part 3: Remembering Our Users 115

Chapter 7   Gophr Part 4: Images 141

Preface

The Internet is a place of constant evolution and creation. Nearly every day, web developers have new tools available to add to their repertoire. In recent years, though, few have been as influential as the Go programming language. Originally created at Google to solve system administration problems, Go has evolved into a modern, powerful, and well-adopted language. To call Go just a language would be a disservice, however; Go is more than a language—it's an entire ecosystem. From the tools that come with it, to the community of developers that build on it, Go is a force majeure in the web development world and it is here to stay.

So what is Go? Well, it's a combination of a strongly typed programming language, and a collection of tools that make working with the language a pleasure. While many may consider a language to comprise merely the syntax, the tools provided to aid development are just as important—if not more so—as the language itself. I hope that as you work through this book you'll see this for yourself, and learn to love Go as I do.

The topics covered in this book are targeted at web development. While Go wasn't created as a "language for web development," it was produced with such a powerful and diverse standard library that web developers have taken to the language in droves, with many organizations now having Go applications powering their services. In this book, we won't be covering every aspect of the standard library; instead we'll be diving deeply into how to create fast, powerful, and maintainable web applications.

Who Should Read This Book

This book assumes at least a basic understanding of many programming and web development principles. If you're unfamiliar with programming, or lack an understanding of how to program for the Web, you may find the concepts discussed in this book hard to grasp. If, however, you're a seasoned web developer, I hope that by seeing Go in action you'll be inspired to try building "the next big thing" in Go.

Conventions Used

You'll notice that we've used certain typographic and layout styles throughout the book to signify different types of information. Look out for the following items:

Code Samples

Code in this book will be displayed using a fixed-width font, like so:

```
<h1>A Perfect Summer's Day</h1>
<p>It was a lovely day for a walk in the park. The birds
were singing and the kids were all back at school.</p>
```

If the code is to be found in the book's code archive, the name of the file will appear at the top of the program listing, like this:

```
                                                          example.css
.footer {
  background-color: #CCC;
  border-top: 1px solid #333;
}
```

If only part of the file is displayed, this is indicated by the word *excerpt*:

```
                                                    example.css (excerpt)
  border-top: 1px solid #333;
```

If additional code is to be inserted into an existing example, the new code will be displayed in bold:

```
function animate() {
  new_variable = "Hello";
}
```

Where existing code is required for context, rather than repeat all the code, a vertical ellipsis will be displayed:

```
function animate() {
    ⋮
    return new_variable;
}
```

Some lines of code are intended to be entered on one line, but we've had to wrap them because of page constraints. A ➥ indicates a line break that exists for formatting purposes only, and should be ignored:

```
URL.open("http://www.sitepoint.com/blogs/2015/05/28/user-style-she
➥ets-come-of-age/");
```

Tips, Notes, and Warnings

 ### Hey, You!

Tips will give you helpful little pointers.

 ### Ahem, Excuse Me ...

Notes are useful asides that are related—but not critical—to the topic at hand. Think of them as extra tidbits of information.

 ### Make Sure You Always ...

... pay attention to these important points.

 ### Watch Out!

Warnings will highlight any gotchas that are likely to trip you up along the way.

Supplementary Materials

http://www.learnable.com/books/go1/
The book's website, which contains links, updates, resources, and more.

https://github.com/spbooks/go1/
The downloadable code archive for this book.

http://community.sitepoint.com/

SitePoint's forums, for help on any tricky web problems.

books@sitepoint.com

Our email address, should you need to contact us for support, to report a problem, or for any other reason.

Some Notes

HTTP Requests

In many of the examples in this book, the intersting part of what's happening is less about what a browser is displaying and more about the way the browser interacts with a web server. We're interested in seeing what data was sent in the request, such as the path we requested, and what headers we sent. In the response, we're interested in what data comes back, not just in the response body, but also the headers that come back.

In most of these cases, instead of showing a screenshot of a browser, I'll simply show the raw HTTP request and response. It's definitely not as pretty, but it's a concise and clear way to get the data that I'm discussing onto the page. Don't worry, there will still be plenty of screenshots.

As an example, here's what a request and response to the SitePoint website looks like:

```
GET / HTTP/1.1

HTTP/1.0 200 OK
Date: Mon, 01 Jun 2015 09:37:11 GMT
Server: Apache/2.2.22 (Debian)
Last-Modified: Mon, 01 Jun 2015 09:36:07 GMT
Expires: Mon, 01 Jun 2015 10:36:07 GMT
Content-Type: text/html; charset=UTF-8
Connection: close

<!-- Page Content Omitted -->
```

Generally I'll avoid leaving any headers in the response that have no significance to what we're talking about.

You can generate your own requests from the command line by using the `curl` tool (you can download curl[1] if you don't already have it). For example, requesting SitePoint with curl would look like this: `curl -i www.sitepoint.com`. This is a great way to inspect what's really going on under the hood.

Go Get

The **go get** tool is a very convenient package manager, but it's also limited in functionality compared to a lot of package managers. When it fetches a package, it has no concept of version, in other words, it will get the latest version of the code you're asking for. While this isn't much of an issue when you're working on your local machine. It means there's a chance that when you go to run your code on another machine, such as during deployment, or if you're part of a team, the new machine might download a different version of the package. Because of this, code that builds on your machine may not build on another machine because you're running different versions of the packages.

There are a few ways to get around this, and we'll cover the options in a later chapter, but for the moment, be aware that if you are getting build errors that appear to originate from another package, it might be because the version you've downloaded is slightly different to the version I used when writing the code for this book. Whenever I introduce a new third party package, I will also note what version of that code I'm using, so if you're comfortable with Git you can navigate to the library and check out the exact same version.

Formatting

There is a standard for how you should format your Go code, and although the compiler won't throw an error if you format your code differently, it's nice to follow the standards. You can completely automate this process by using the tool `gofmt` that comes with the Go installation. This tool will automatically reformat your Go code for you. All popular text editors will have a plugin that automatically runs `gofmt` for you when you save your files. I highly recommend taking the time to install one for your editor — trust me, it'll be one of the best things you ever do.

---

[1] http://curl.haxx.se/dlwiz/?type=bin

Imports

Most code examples will only show the relevant parts of the code, and aren't compilable on their own. Don't worry, the code download contains compilable versions of each code example. If you're writing the code as you read the book, the most important thing to note is that you'll need to be importing the packages that are used.

Imports can turn into a hassle, as it's not only a compile time error to use a library that isn't imported, but it's also an error to build code that imports a library that isn't used. You'll quickly find yourself getting annoyed at having to add and remove import lines from you files. Luckily the Go community knows this, and there is a tool called `goimports`[2] that will automatically add and remove import lines from your code as required. Most editor plugins that run `gofmt` will also handle `goimports`.

Guiding Gently, Not Explicitly

In some areas of the code, I will explain a few alternative methods for achieving a goal. Often there will be some trade-offs or advantages for one way or another, and I will attempt to explain these. I do this because frequently there's no right or wrong way to do something. A choice is often a matter of personal preference, or may depend on the specific project requirements. Because of this, I think it's best that I cover a few options, rather than make a choice for you.

Terminal

Throughout this book I'll use the term "terminal" to refer to your command line. Some users may have custom terminals installed, so feel free to use whatever you're comfortable with. If you don't have a preference, or aren't familiar with the concept, all systems will come with an application you can use. Mac users should use Terminal.app, Linux users will also have a terminal as part of their distribution, and Windows users can use cmd.exe.

---

[2] http://godoc.org/golang.org/x/tools/cmd/goimports

Want to take your learning further?

Thanks for choosing to buy a SitePoint book. Do you want to continue learning? You can now gain unlimited access to courses and ALL SitePoint books at Learnable for one low price. Enroll now and start learning today! Join Learnable and you'll stay ahead of the newest technology trends: http://www.learnable.com.

Chapter 1

Welcome New Gopher

This chapter is designed to give you a grounding in the fundamentals of the Go language. We'll start out by covering installation on various operating systems and write our first piece of Go code, before moving on to look at Go's tools, syntax, and types. Let's get started!

Installation

The first step in writing Go code is to get your hands on the Go tool set, available at https://golang.org/doc/install. The Go authors provide installation packages for Windows, Mac OS, and Linux. You can also install Go from the source code, and if you're on a system other than those with pre-built installers, you'll need to do it this way.

Once installed, you should be able to type `go version` in your command line and see your Go version printed. If there's an error, try reopening your command line software again; otherwise, refer to the Go website[1] for troubleshooting.

---

[1] http://golang.org/

Alias Golang

Go's main website is golang.org, and the language is quite often referred to as "Golang." If you're having trouble searching when using the term "Go," try using "Golang" instead, as it's a little less ambiguous. They're one and the same.

The Go Workspace

Throughout this book, you'll see examples of why Go is referred to as an "opinionated" programming language, and the way you should lay out your development workspace is one of them. Where other languages might allow you to set up your projects however you wish, Go likes you to do it Go's way, which in this instance is to keep all your code within a specific directory structure inside a directory known as your **GOPATH**. This enables Go to provide tools that let you easily download and manage third-party source code; without it, you'll be unable to use any libraries except for the standard ones that come with Go.

This may be at odds to your regular way of working, but give it a chance. I fought it at first, but have since learned to accept the "Go way," and now find it to be a common sense approach to code management.

Your **GOPATH** will contains several directories, the most important of which is the **src** directory. This is where you'll write your code, and where Go will install third-party source code. Create a directory on your computer now, and place an **src** directory inside it.When you want to write some Go code, it should be in a directory inside **src**. To tell Go what directory the **GOPATH** is, we'll set an environment variable of the same name. If you're unfamiliar with environment variables, they're a way of providing system configuration values, and are available on Windows, Linux, and Mac OS systems.

Mac OS and Linux

To add an environment variable in Mac OS or Linux, you'll need to add it to your Bash profile, which is loaded every time you run a terminal window:

```
echo "export GOPATH=~/Gocode" >> ~/.bash_profile
source ~/.bash_profile
```

This sets the directory **Gocode** in your home directory as your GOPATH and reloads the configuration.

 Alternative Shells

If you don't use Bash, these instructions may fail to work. If you've installed an alternative shell, such as zsh, consult the instructions for that software or google it. Actually, if you've installed your own shell, chances are you already know how to do this.

Windows

The environment variables menu is available in Windows 8 by right-clicking the bottom-left of the screen from the desktop, selecting **System**, then **Advanced System Settings**, then the **Advanced** tab, then the **Environment Variables** button. You can see it in Figure 1.1.

In Windows 7 and Windows Vista, right-click the **Computer** icon on the desktop or the **Computer** option in the **Start** menu. Select **Properties** and then **Advanced System Settings**, the **Advanced** tab, then the **Environment Variables** button.

Figure 1.1. The environment variables menu in Windows

Once you're in the environment variables menu, select **New...** in the **System Variables** area and create a new variable called `GOPATH` with the location of your Go workspace as the value, as seen in Figure 1.2. In my examples, I've used `C:\Gocode`.

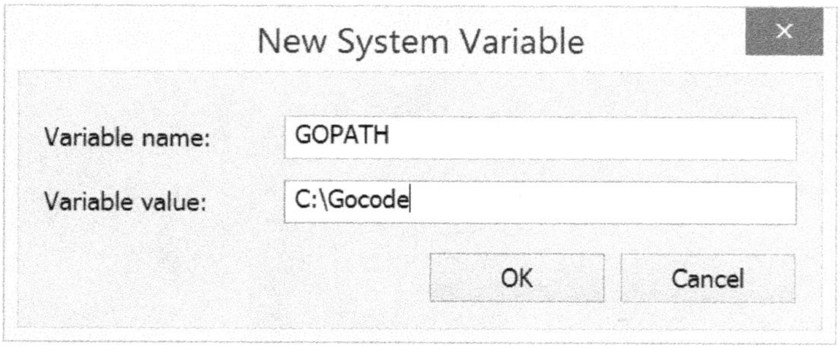

Figure 1.2. Creating a new system variable

Your First Go Code

This chapter will introduce the basics of the Go syntax as well as some of the standard tools we'll be using to write our code. Rather than a comprehensive guide to the Go language, it's an introduction to set you up with some foundation knowledge. As we progress through the book, we'll introduce more concepts when we come across them.

Any good programming book start with a basic "Hello World" example, so let's follow in the footsteps of giants, in order to get our feet wet with some Go. Create a new file, **helloworld.go**, and enter the following code:

```
helloworld.go

package main

import "fmt"

func main() {
    fmt.Println("Hello World")
}
```

Now in your terminal from the same directory, you can tell Go to run your code:

```
go run helloworld.go
```

If your code runs successfully, you should see `Hello World` printed in your terminal. This is an elementary program but includes the basic structure of most Go applications. To start, we declare the package name to which this code belongs. A **package** is the way we group related code, and `main` is a special package that defines code to be executed directly. If you wanted to create a package to use in another Go program, you'd add a unique package name here. We'll cover writing your own packages in a later chapter.

Next up we import the packages that we'll use. Since this is a simple program, it just imports one package: `fmt`. The `fmt` package is part of the Go standard library that comes with the Go tools we've downloaded. It's capable of performing basic formatting and printing operations. Since `fmt` is part of the standard library, it's a very basic import statement. Later on, we'll see how Go handles importing third-party packages from source control by including just a URL in the import statement; for example, import "github.com/tools/godep".

Lastly we have a function called main, which calls the function Println in the fmt package. The main function is the entry point to your application, and will be run when your program starts. Println simply prints out a value, and you can pass as many variables as you'd like.

At this point you may have noticed a few characteristics about the Go syntax. Firstly, its parenthesis and curly braces look like many C-derivative languages. Secondly, there's a noticeable lack of semicolons; new lines are commonly used to determine the end of one statement and the beginning of the next. Finally, you might have noticed that it takes a relatively short time to compile or run your code. This is one of the decisions the Go team made early on—that Go would sacrifice a little on the performance side to ensure the code compiles quickly, and that goes a long way towards making the language an enjoyable one in which to develop.

Go Tools

We've seen the first example of the Go tools. We've used the go command line tool to run our code. go run compiles and runs the code. And if we wanted to create an executable program instead of merely running the program, we could run go build. The build command will create an executable binary file named after the current directory, and build all the files in the directory; there's no need to tell it which files to build. For example, I have my helloworld.go file in a directory chapter1. If I run go build, I will have an executable file chapter1 created inside that directory. We can take this one step further with the go install tool, which will build the file and then place the executable into your $GOPATH/bin directory. If you add that directory to your system's PATH environment variable, you'll be able to install your Go program and run it from anywhere in your system.

PATH Environment Variable

Your PATH is a list of directories in which your system looks for executable programs. When you run any command on your system, it will search each of these directories (in order) for a command of that name, and run the first one it finds—or complain that you don't have it! On Windows, you can edit the PATH settings in the same area you set up your GOPATH. On Mac OS or Linux, you can use the same method as earlier to add `export PATH=$PATH:$GOPATH/bin` to your Bash profile, which will append the directory to the `PATH`.

Basic Types

Go is a **strongly typed** language. What this means is that any variable can only hold a single type of value, so sometimes you'll need to convert between types. Once a variable has been assigned a type, it can only hold that particular type. Go provides a variety of primitive types, along with the ability for you to create your own types that extend these primitives.

Strings

One of the most common primitive types is the **string**. Let's look at how we'd create a new variable that holds a string:

```
myString := "I'm a string."
```

Notice how we assign the string to the variable `myString` by using a colon followed by an equals sign, `:=`. This is how we initialize a new variable. If we want to change the string stored in `myValue` after it's initialized, we can omit the colon. In fact, if we were to include it, the program wouldn't compile:

```
myString := "I'm a string."
myString = "I'm really a string, I promise."
```

If you tried to reinitialize the variable, you'd receive an error that says "no new variables on left side of :=" when attempting to compile your code.

To concatenate strings, you can use the + operator:

```
myString := "I'm a string."
myOtherString := myString + " I really am."
fmt.Println(myOtherString) // Outputs "I'm a string. I really am."
```

 Commenting in Go

Both single-line and multiple-line comments are available in Go. Single-line comments start with a //, and multiple-line comments are surrounded by /* and */.

Numbers

Go has a variety of categories for representing numbers. There are two categories of numbers that we'll be looking at: integers and floating-point numbers. An **integer** is a whole number without a decimal component, such as 1, -7, and 42. A **floating-point number**, or **float**, can contain a decimal component, such as 3.141 or -9.2.

Integers

Within each category of number, there are several types. Integers have the most types: `int`, `int8`, `int16`, `int32`, `int64`, `uint`, `uint8`, `uint16`, `uint32`, and `uint64`. Each type is capable of holding different sets of numbers based on how many bits of memory the variable is stored in (8, 16, 32, or 64). For example, an `int8` is capable of holding numbers from -128 to 127, while an `int64` is capable of holding from -9223372036854775808 to 9223372036854775807. Any type starting with `int` is a signed integer, which can represent both negative and positive numbers, and those starting with `uint` are unsigned, and can only hold positive numbers.

If you know the maximum value range you'll assign to a variable you can choose a more appropriate type, since it will reduce the memory assigned to store the variable; however, you'll find that in most instances you'll be using an `int64` or `int` type.

 int Type Is Special

The `int` type is special, and its size will depend on the architecture of the computer you're using. In practice most systems will be running a 64-bit architecture, and `int` will be the same as an `int64`. This also applies to the `uint` type.

Floats

There are only two floating point types, `float32` and `float64`. Using a `float64` over a `float32` increases its precision, whether that's a larger number or more decimal places.

You cannot perform operations on variables that contain different types. If you attempt to, you'll incur an error along the lines of "invalid operation: a * b (mismatched types int and float64)." You can change between numeric types by performing a type conversion:

```
myInt := 2
myFloat := 1.5
myOtherFloat := float64(myInt) * myFloat
fmt.Println(myOtherFloat) // Outputs 3
```

 Type Conversion

To convert a type, commonly called "casting" in other languages, you pass the variable into parenthesis after the target type. This will only work with types of the same category, as these numbers are; if you try to convert between incompatible types you'll get a compiler error. We'll see some more examples of type conversion later on.

Booleans

The **bool** type represents a value that is one of two predefined constants: `true` or `false`. There's little more to say about it than that—other than they're great for conditionals:

```
myBool := true
if myBool {
    fmt.Println("myBool is true")
} else {
    fmt.Println("myBool isn't true")
}
```

Arrays and Slices

Arrays are an interesting subject in Go. Most of the time you'll be dealing with **slices**, which refers to part or all of an underlying array, and is analogous to an array in most programming languages. Because in almost all day-to-day programming you'll be dealing with slices, I'll skip covering more about arrays, but if you're interesting in learning about the underlying data type of slices, I recommend reading the article "Go Slices: usage and internals" by the Go team.[2]

Slices are defined in the form []T where T is the type being stored in the slice. Only values of a single type can be stored in a slice. Let's look at how we can create a slice, and also make further slices from a slice (by slicing it!):

```go
mySlice := []int{1, 2, 3, 4, 5}
mySlice2 := mySlice[0:3]
mySlice3 := mySlice[1:4]
fmt.Println(mySlice2, mySlice3, mySlice[2])
// Outputs: [1 2 3] [2 3 4] 3
```

First, we create a slice of type int that contains five values. The curly brackets are Go's way of instantiating a new instance of the type that precedes it. You'll be seeing it a lot.

After we've created our slice, we're able to create other slices from it. The colon notation inside the square brackets refers to a start and end index that should be used to create the slice. A single index number inside square brackets refers to a single element in the slice. If you attempt to use an index that's outside the bounds of a slice, you'll get an error along the lines of "panic: runtime error: index out of range" when your code runs. As per most programming languages, the first index in a slice is number 0 rather than 1.

 Runtime versus Compile Time Errors

> The compiler understands a lot about our programs, and will often refuse to compile if we try to perform a task that we shouldn't. If you try to access an invalid index on a slice, however, this is a runtime error, since Go is unable to infer at compile time what the size of the slice will be (as they are dynamically sized, they can change size). As a result, you should always be careful about accessing a value in a slice by checking its length.

If we want to know the length of a slice, we can use the built-in len function:

---

[2] http://blog.golang.org/go-slices-usage-and-internals

```
mySlice := []int{1, 2, 3, 4, 5}
fmt.Println(len(mySlice)) // Outputs: 5

mySlice := []string{"Hi", "there"}
fmt.Println(len(mySlice)) // Outputs: 2
```

Looping

To iterate over a slice, we use a `for` statement with a `range` clause:

```
animals := []string{"Cat", "Dog", "Emu", "Warthog"}
for i, animal := range animals {
    fmt.Println(animal, "is at index", i)
}
```

This will output:

```
Cat is at index 0
Dog is at index 1
Emu is at index 2
Warthog is at index 3
```

If we didn't want to use the index value i, for example, we can't just assign it and ignore it. We'd receive the error "i declared and not used". If there are no plans to use a certain value, it must be assigned to the **blank identifier**, represented by an underscore (_). The blank identifier is how we discard a value that we have no use for:

```
animals := []string{"Cat", "Dog", "Emu", "Warthog"}
for _, animal := range animals {
    fmt.Println(animal)
}
```

Maps

Go provides a **map** type that lets us assign key/value pairs to it. This type is analogous to a hash table in other languages, or an object in JavaScript. To create a map, we assign a type for both the key and the value, such as `map[string]int`. For example, if we wanted to store the years that the Star Wars movies were released, we could create a map such as this:

```go
starWarsYears := map[string]int{
    "A New Hope":             1977,
    "The Empire Strikes Back": 1980,
    "Return of the Jedi":     1983,
    "Attack of the Clones":   2002,
    "Revenge of the Sith":    2005,
}
```

If you wanted to add another value into the map, we can do so this way:

```go
starWarsYears["The Force Awakens"] = 2015
```

Note that the := operator is not used.

As with slices, you can ascertain the length of a map with the `len` function:

```go
fmt.Println(len(starWarsMovies)) // Correctly outputs: 6
```

Looping over Maps

Looping over maps is very similar to interating over slices. We use a `for` loop with a `range` clause, and this time instead of the index integer as the first assigned value, we get the key:

```go
for title, year := range starWarsYears {
        fmt.Println(title, "was released in", year)
}
```

If you run this code, you'll see an output along the lines of this:

```
Revenge of the Sith was released in 2005
The Force Awakens was released in 2015
A New Hope was released in 1977
```

```
The Empire Strikes Back was released in 1980
Return of the Jedi was released in 1983
Attack of the Clones was released in 2002
```

If you run it again, the values will output in a different order. It's important to understand that unlike arrays and slices, maps are not output in any particular order. In fact, to ensure that developers are aware of this, maps are ordered randomly when ranged over.

Dealing with Map Values

We can get a value associated with a key by passing the key inside square brackets:

```
colours := map[string]string{
    "red":     "#ff0000",
    "green":   "#00ff00",
    "blue":    "#0000ff",
    "fuchsia": "#ff00ff",
}
redHexCode := colours["red"]
```

It's worth noting that the variable redHexCode would be assigned the "empty value" of the map's type if the key didn't exist—in this case, that's an empty string.

If you want to delete a value from a map, you can use the built-in delete function:

```
delete(colours, "fuchsia")
```

The delete function won't return anything, and also does nothing if the key you've specified fails to exist. If you want to know if a key exists you can use the special two-value assignment, where the second value is a Boolean that represents whether the key exists or not:

```
code, exists := colours["burgundy"]
if exists {
    fmt.Println("Burgundy's hex code is", code)
```

```
} else {
    fmt.Println("I don't know burgundy")
}
```

Functions

We've already seen an example of a function in the Hello World excercise at the start of the chapter. Let's have a look at functions in a bit more depth.

A **function** is defined with the keyword func, and can take multiple parameters and return multiple values. Each parameter and return value has to have a type specified; if sequential parameters are of the same type, you can just add the type definition to the last parameter of that type. Here are a few examples:

```
func noParamsNoReturn() {
    fmt.Println("I'm not really doing much!")
}

func twoParamsOneReturn(myInt int, myString string) string {
    return fmt.Sprintf("myInt: %d, myString: %s", myInt, myString)
}

func oneParamTwoReturns(myInt int) (string, int) {
    return fmt.Sprintf("Int: %d", myInt), myInt + 1
}

func twoSameTypedParams(myString1, myString2 string) {
    fmt.Println("String 1", myString1)
    fmt.Println("String 2", myString2)
}
```

In the first example, we see a function with no parameters or return values; this is the simplest function you can create. twoParamsOneReturn shows a function that takes two parameters of different types and returns a single string value. oneParamTwoReturns takes a single integer parameter, and returns both a string and an integer. Lastly, twoSameTypedParams shows how we can take two parameters of the same type and only need to add the type information to the last parameter of that type.

Handling functions that return multiple values is as simple as providing comma-separated variables in which to place the values. We could use the `oneParamTwoReturns` function this way:

```
func main(){
    a, b := oneParamTwoReturns(3)
    fmt.Println(a) // Outputs "Int: 3"
    fmt.Println(b) // Outputs "4"
}
```

A lot of functions will return two values: one for the actual response from the function and a second to indicate whether or not an error has occurred. This is a very common practice in Go and forms the basis for handling errors, which we'll cover later. While you can return more than two values, it's not common to see this.

Pointers

When you pass a variable to a function, it receives a copy of the variable, rather than the variable itself. If you alter a variable inside the function, the code that called the function will fail to see those changes.

Pointers allow you to pass a reference to an object, rather than the object itself. This means that you can alter the underlying object, and other areas of your code will see the updated value rather than a function altering a copy. If you're coming from a language that supports pointers, sometimes called "passing by reference", you'll be familiar with this concept.

Pointers are best explained by this common everyday scenario: You have a banana, a pear, a fruit storage locker, and a cloning machine. You create a variable `myFruit` and place a banana in it, then pass that variable into the cloning machine. The variable that comes out of the cloning machine, `myClonedFruit` then has the pear put into it. Now `myFruit` has a banana and `myClonedFruit` has a pear. Changing `myClonedFruit` has no effect on `myFruit`.

As you might have guessed, this is what happens when we pass a variable directly into a function. It creates a new variable for that function, which is a copy, and altering it has no effect on the original variable.

Now let's look at what happens when we make use of our fruit storage locker. We'll start from scratch, so forget about the previous variables. We create a variable `myFruit` and place the banana in it. We then place the variable in the fruit locker, send the location of the fruit locker to the cloning machine, and receive a new variable myC-lonedFruit. This time we haven't copied the fruit, we've copied the location of the fruit—the fruit locker. We then put the pear in the fruit locker. We now have two variables, myFruit and myClonedFruit, which both have a pear in them, because they're both in the same fruit locker.

In this second example, instead of passing a fruit variable into the function, we've passed a pointer to a fruit variable. This pointer points to the address in memory where the fruit is stored, so when we change the value at that address, both the function and the calling code are referencing the same value.

So what does this actually look like in Go? Let's check out an example:

```go
func giveMePear(fruit string) {
    fruit = "pear"
}

func main() {
    fruit := "banana"
    giveMePear(fruit)
    fmt.Println(fruit) // Outputs: banana
}
```

This example passes the fruit variable into the giveMePear function, which receives a copy of the fruit and then assigns it:

```go
func giveMePear(fruit *string) {
    *fruit = "pear"
}

func main() {
    fruit := "banana"
    giveMePear(&fruit)
    fmt.Println(fruit) // Outputs: pear
}
```

In the second example, instead of taking a string as a parameter, the giveMePear function accepts a pointer to a string—denoted with a *string. Inside the function we assign a new string into the value that the pointer references, again using the * symbol. When we call the function, instead of just passing in the variable fruit, we take the address of the variable. We do this by prepending the variable with an ampersand, &. This tells Go that we have no interest in the variable itself, just a pointer to the variable, which is where that variable is in memory.

At this point, don't worry if you're struggling to fully understand the concept of pointers. We'll see them in action soon, and it is hoped you'll build up an understanding as we continue on through the book.

 nil Pointers

One element to note when using pointers is that there's no guarantee you'll have a value passed into the function. You could also pass in `nil`, which represents no value (note, this is very different to `false`, which only applies to Boolean values). While it's obvious in our example that we're not passing nil into the function, more often than not you're using variables that have been passed through from other areas of the code, so you must check whether a value is actually passed. If you try to access or alter a nil pointer, you'll receive an error along the lines of "panic: runtime error: invalid memory address or nil pointer dereference". You can avoid this error by checking if the variable is equal to `nil` in situations where a nil value may be passed.

Structs

Go allows you to define your own types, and most custom types you write will be structs. A **struct** is a type that contains named fields. If we continue with the movie example from earlier, we might create a `Movie` type that has some data associated with it:

```
type Movie struct {
    Actors      []string
    Rating      float32
    ReleaseYear int
    Title       string
}
```

As you can see we've created a variety of fields, each with their own associated type. You'll see that the field names start with an uppercase letter. This is very important, and means that those values can be accessed by code outside the package in which the type was defined. These fields are referred to as being exported, and we'll cover the practical realities of exported and unexported code in a later chapter. While not exactly analogous, you can think of an exported field or method as being "public" rather than "private."

To create an instance of the `Movie` type, we use the curly brackets like when we created slices and maps:

```
episodeIV := Movie{
    Title:       "Star Wars: A New Hope",
    Rating:      5.0,
    ReleaseYear: 1977,
}
```

We now have an instance of the `Movie` type stored in `episodeIV`. We only supplied three of the four fields, so the fourth field `Actors` will be instantiated with the empty value for its type—in this case, `nil`.

We're able to access the fields through dot notation, and can read and assign the fields just like with already instantiated variables:

```
episodeIV.Actors = []string{
    "Mark Hamill",
    "Harrison Ford",
    "Carrie Fisher",
}
fmt.Println(episodeIV.Title, "has a rating of", episodeIV.Rating)
```

Type Methods

You can add your own methods to any types you define. This is as easy as defining a function that has what's called a receiver type. A **receiver type** is similar to a single parameter definition in a function, but is declared just after the `func` keyword but before the function name. If we wanted to define a method that formatted a movie title for display, along with the movie's release year, we could create a `DisplayTitle` method like so:

```
func (movie Movie) DisplayTitle() string {
    return fmt.Sprintf("%s (%d)", movie.Title, movie.ReleaseYear)
}
```

```
func main() {
    episodeV := Movie{
        Title:       "Star Wars: The Empire Strikes Back",
        ReleaseYear: 1980,
    }
    fmt.Println(episodeV.DisplayTitle())
    // Outputs: "Star Wars: The Empire Strikes Back (1980)"
}
```

You'll see that before the function name, `DisplayTitle`, we declare a receiver type of (`movie Movie`). This gives us a variable `movie` of type `Movie` that we can access just like any other function parameter. This might take some getting your head around, as it means there's no concept of "this" or "self" as you see in other strongly object-oriented languages.

 Object-oriented Programming in Go

Receiver functions are the basis for object-oriented programming in Go, in that a type with various methods is analogous to an object in most object-oriented languages. I must stress that Go doesn't provide a lot of the traditional object-oriented programming constructs, such as inheritance, but this is by design. Go provides various methods for creating complex data types, such as embedded types and interfaces, which we'll cover soon.

Receiver types can also refer to a pointer of a type. Without a pointer, any changes that you make to the instance will fail to make it any further than the end of the method. A straightforward example of this might be a counter type with a method `Increment` that adds one to a count field:

```
type Counter struct {
    Count int
}

func (c Counter) Increment() {
    c.Count++
}

func (c *Counter) IncrementWithPointer() {
    c.Count++
}
```

```
func main() {
    counter := &Counter{}
    fmt.Println(counter.Count) // Outputs: 0

    counter.Increment()
    fmt.Println(counter.Count) // Outputs: 0

    counter.IncrementWithPointer()
    fmt.Println(counter.Count) // Outputs: 1
}
```

As you can see when we call the `Increment` method, which only receives a copy of the instance, the field `Count` is not incremented outside the scope of the `Increment` method. The method that receives the pointer to the object, however, alters the same `Counter` instance, and we see the change outside the `IncrementWithPointer` method. It's interesting to note that we immediately took the address of the `Counter` instance with the `&` symbol, and that we were able to call both the method with and without the pointer receiver type. This will not work in reverse: if we failed to take the address and just said `counter := Counter{}`, we'd be unable to call the method `IncrementWithPointer`.

Exported and Unexported Code

When writing your own packages and structs, you need to decide what methods, functions, constants, and fields will be available to code outside the package. An **exported** value is available to code outside the package, **unexported** values are not. If you're unsure whether or not some code should be exported, it's a good rule of thumb to make it unexported, then change the name if you realize it's required outside the package:

```
// myUnexportedFunc is not available to code outside this package
func myUnexportedFunc() {
}

// MyExportedFunc is available outside this package, though
func MyExportedFunc() {
}

type MyExportedType struct{
```

```
    ExportedField    string
    unexportedField  string
}
```

Summary

That covers our introduction to the basics of the Go syntax and types. In the next chapter, we'll look at creating our own types, how to create interfaces that serve as a contract for other types to implement, and how Go handles third-party libraries.

Chapter **2**

Go Types Explored

In the last chapter, we were introduced to the basic Go types and syntax. In this chapter we'll go a little deeper into some of the types, and how to define your own types and interfaces. We'll also cover how Go lets us use third-party libraries in our software with ease.

Custom Types

While you can't add your own methods to built-in types, you can create your own types from other types. A common example of this is a `ByteSize` type, which extends `float64` and provides a custom formatted string to represent a size in bytes such as 2 kilobytes or 3.14 megabytes:

```
const (
    KB = 1024
    MB = KB * 1024
    GB = MB * 1024
    TB = GB * 1024
    PB = TB * 1024
)
```

```
type ByteSize float64

func (b ByteSize) String() string {
    switch {
    case b >= PB:
        return "Very Big"
    case b >= TB:
        return fmt.Sprintf("%.2fTB", b/TB)
    case b >= GB:
        return fmt.Sprintf("%.2fGB", b/GB)
    case b >= MB:
        return fmt.Sprintf("%.2fMB", b/MB)
    case b >= KB:
        return fmt.Sprintf("%.2fKB", b/KB)
    }
    return fmt.Sprintf("%dB", b)
}

func main(){
    fmt.Println(ByteSize(2048)) // Outputs: 2.00KB
    fmt.Println(ByteSize(3292528.64)) // Outputs: 3.14MB
}
```

First, we've defined some constants that represent the various sizes of a kilobyte, megabyte, and so on. A constant is just like a variable, except once defined it cannot be changed.

Next up, we create a new type `Bytesize` that uses `float64` as a base. We then define a new method `String` that returns a string, and in that method we check against the size of the value compared to our constants. We're using a `select` statement, and the first `case` that matches will return a nicely formatted string that's reduced down to just two decimal places, plus a suffix. A select statement is just like multiple `if else` statements, but it's a little tidier for this use case.

In our `main` function we create a couple of `ByteSize` instances and pass them to `fmt.Println`. You'll notice that nowhere do we actually call the `String` method. This is because the `fmt` package knows to use the `String` method if it exists on a type. This might seem a little magical, but all will be revealed in the next section!

Elegant Constants With Iota

Did defining the constants for kilobytes and gigabytes seem a little long-winded? Fortunately, Go provides a syntax for defining incrementing constants called **iota**. It starts at zero and counts up. For example, we could define the numbers one through five like so:

```
const(
    one int = iota + 1
    two
    ⋮
)
```

We only need to define the type and iota expression for the first constant, and then each subsequent constant will re-evaluate the expression with the next value of iota. We can use a slightly more complicated expression to define our byte constants:

```
const(
    KB ByteSize = 1<<(10*(iota+1))
    MB
    GB
    TB
    PB
)
```

Here we're using the *left shift* operator << to create the appropriate sizes. Understanding this operator can be tricky, but think of it as: multiply the number on the left by 2 X times, where X is the number on the right. So in the first case, 1 is multiplied by 2 ten times—creating 1,024 for KB, and in the second case, 1 is multiplied by 2 twenty times—creating 1,048,576 for MB.

Interfaces

Go provides a powerful "shared data type" paradigm through its interface model. An **interface** is a type defined with a specific set of method signatures, and any type that matches the method signatures implicitly implements the interface; there's no need to explicitly declare that you're implementing "interface X". This is best explained with an example, so let's jump right into one:

```go
type Fruit interface {
    String() string
}

type Apple struct {
    Variety string
}

func (a Apple) String() string {
    return fmt.Sprintf("A %s apple", a.Variety)
}

type Orange struct {
    Size string
}

func (o Orange) String() string {
    return fmt.Sprintf("A %s orange", o.Size)
}

func PrintFruit(fruit Fruit) {
    fmt.Println("I have this fruit:", fruit.String())
}

func main() {
    apple := Apple{"Golden Delicious"}
    orange := Orange{"large"}

    PrintFruit(apple)
    PrintFruit(orange)
}
```

```
I have this fruit: A Golden Delicious apple
I have this fruit: A large orange
```

Here we've defined an interface type Fruit, which requires a single method to be implemented: String() string. This method takes no parameters and returns a string, so any type with a String method that returns a string will be considered to implement Fruit. After that we've created two new struct types, Apple and Orange, both of which have different fields but implement the String method correctly. These types both implement Fruit. Lastly, we've created a function that takes a Fruit instance and prints out the result of the String method. In our main function we create an `orange` and an `apple`, then pass them to the `PrintFruit` function. It's important to note that the variables `apple` and `orange` have types of `Apple` and `Orange` respectively. Only when they're passed into the function `PrintFruit` is their type `Fruit`.

The power of interfaces is in that the calling code is unaffected by what the underlying type or implementation, as long as it match the method signatures. This is powerful when writing packages that are designed for reuse.

Let's look at a new hypothetical situation: Say you sell a web application that offers a product catalog. At first your customers only have a few products to sell, so you just store the information in a file and load it when the application runs. Then you have a customer with a large amount of products, so it's time to move the products into a database of some sort. If you want to use the same codebase to handle the products but abstract away the details of where the products are stored and retrieved from, you could define an interface for the product catalogue and then have different implementations for the file catalog and database catalog. We'll skip going into the implementations, but we can look at the general structure of how this might work. First we'd create an interface to define what methods we're dealing with for a product catalog:

```
type ProductCatalogue interface {
    All() ([]Product, error)
    Find(string) (Product, error)
}
```

This sets us up to handle getting all of the products and getting just a specific product—the general requirement for a small ecommerce website. There might be more methods required, but I'll keep this example minimal. Next up we'll define the actual implementations of the interface—for the file storage and for some database storage:

```
type FileProductCatalogue struct {
    … // Some fields would be here, perhaps the file location
}

func (c FileProductCatalogue) All() ([]Product, error) {
    … // Implementation omitted
}
```

```go
func (c FileProductCatalogue) Find(id string) (Product, error) {
    … // Implementation omitted
}

type DBProductCatalogue struct {
    … // Some fields would be here, perhaps a database connection
}

func (c DBProductCatalogue) All() ([]Product, error) {
    … // Implementation omitted
}

func (c DBProductCatalogue) Find(id string) (Product, error) {
    … // Implementation omitted
}
```

Now we have two very different implementations of the same interface. One that loads from a file and one that loads from a database. When we're creating a variable, we can do so with a type of `ProductCatalogue` rather than the specific implementation:

```go
func main() {
    var myCatalogue ProductCatalogue
    myCatalogue = DBProductCatalogue{}
    …
}
```

Or we could have an initialization function that accepts any `ProductCatalogue` implementation:

```go
func LoadProducts(catalogue ProductCatalogue) {
    products, err := catalogue.All()
    …
}
```

 ## Multiple Interfaces

A type isn't limited to implementing a single interface. For example, the `Fruit` interface we saw in the first example is exactly the same as the `Stringer` interface from the `fmt` package. If you pass an instance of `Fruit` to `fmt.Println`, you'll see the result of the `String` method printed.

The most basic interface in the language is the empty interface `interface{}`, which has no methods and therefore every single type implements it. A type has no limits regarding methods that implement interface methods either; all that matters is that the methods the interface requires exist on the type.

Error Handling

Error handling in Go is very much an in-your-face situation. A lot of languages allow you to program without forcing you to think about error handling. You might have the ability to rescue or catch errors, but if you don't want to you don't have to, and your code will fail in interesting ways that are difficult to track.

In Go, the convention is to check for errors everywhere, and therefore be constantly thinking about how you handle them and what they mean. While some might think this is a terrible idea—and it certainly does lead to more code—it results in robust code where error handling is a core part of the functionality rather than an afterthought.

Remember earlier when we saw multiple values being returned from a function? In most cases when you're receiving multiple values, the last value is an error. This means you need to assign the value to a variable (or actively choose to assign it to the blank identifier _ and ignore it), and check that variable. It's very common to see code such as this:

```
someValue, err := doSomething()
if err != nil {
    return err // Handle the error
}
```

After every call to a function that returns an error, there's a check to see whether an error occurred and handling it if it did. More often than not, this means passing it back up the chain for one of the calling functions to handle. While this adds lines to your code, it also makes you think about what were to happen if this code failed to continue on, and consider all the variations of failures that could occur. In a world where a lot of code relies on the availability of external resources, such as network connections and disk availability, it's more important than ever to design for failure, and Go surfaces this with its error handling.

So what exactly is an error? Well, it's a great example of an interface. An error is actually just a normal Go interface, and is any type that implements the `Error` method:

```
type error interface {
    Error() string
}
```

This leads the way for us to create our own error types. We can either extend an existing type, or create a struct with extra data. For example, if we wanted an error type that represents an invalid HTTP status code, we could define our own integer type:

```
type ErrInvalidStatusCode int

func (code ErrInvalidStatusCode) Error() string {
    return fmt.Sprintf("Expected 200 ok, but got %d", code)
}
```

And then if we received an invalid code, we could just convert the code to the type `ErrInvalidStatusCode`:

```
if myStatusCode != 200 {
    return ErrInvalidStatusCode(myStatusCode)
}
```

Embedded Types

Struct types are allowed to have other types embedded in them. This allows for a level of object "inheritance", although it's not quite the same as classic object-oriented inheritance. You embed a type by adding the type to a struct without a field name. The struct then gains access to the embedded value and its methods:

```
type User struct {
    Name string
}
```

```go
func (u User) IsAdmin() bool { return false }
func (u User) DisplayName() string {
    return u.Name
}

type Admin struct {
    User
}
func (a Admin) IsAdmin() bool { return true }
func (a Admin) DisplayName() string {
    // Add [Admin] in front of the embedded user's display name
    return "[Admin] " + a.User.DisplayName()
}

func main() {
    u := User{"Normal User"}
    fmt.Println(u.Name)            // Normal User
    fmt.Println(u.DisplayName())   // Normal User
    fmt.Println(u.IsAdmin())       // false

    a := Admin{User{"Admin User"}}
    fmt.Println(a.Name)            // Admin User
    fmt.Println(a.User.Name)       // Admin User
    fmt.Println(a.DisplayName())   // [Admin] Admin User
    fmt.Println(a.IsAdmin())       // true
}
```

We can see here that the User type is straightforward, but the Admin type has an embedded User. An instance of Admin is able to access the fields and methods of the embedded User as if they were its own. We can see that when we print both the Name and User.Name at the start, they are the exact same thing.

The interesting part happens when we overwrite a method that exists on the embedded type. We see this with the DisplayName method, where we're able to prepend a string to the embedded type's DisplayName method.

Embedding types is very useful when implementing interfaces. If your type has an embedded type that implements an interface, then your type automatically implements that interface too. This is because all the methods of the embedded type are available on the type that embeds it, and the methods are what defines whether or not a type implements an interface.

Distinct from Subclassing

Subclassing in most object-oriented languages means creating a class that extends from another class and inherits all its methods and properties. The main difference is that in these scenarios the parent class and child class share their properties and methods; that is, access goes both ways—from child to parent and parent to child. In Go, however, an embedded type has no awareness of the type in which it's embedded, so it cannot access its fields or methods; thus it only goes one way.

The `defer` Command

The final language feature that we'll look at in this chapter is the `defer` command. This command enables us to tell a function to run after we return from the current function. By deferring a function early on, we can ensure that some functionality runs regardless of where in the function we return, as well as grouping logic together at the place where it makes sense.

An example of this is closing a file in a function. It makes sense to write the code that closes the function right where we open it, and we don't have to think about closing it if we return from the function early:

```go
func CopyFile(dstName, srcName string) error {
    src, err := os.Open(srcName)
    if err != nil {
        return err
    }
    defer src.Close()

    dst, err := os.Open(dstName)
    if err != nil {
        return err
    }
    defer dst.Close()

    _, err := io.Copy(dst, src)
    return err
}
```

In this example, we open two different files so that we can copy from one to the other. By calling `defer src.Close()` after we open the source file, we're saved from having to remember calling it before we return at the end of the function, or when we return if there's an error opening the dst file. This has reduced the amount of code we have to write and made the code more stable. If the function changed and added another block of code that may return from the function early, there's no need to think about closing files.

Third-party Libraries

So far we've only used standard libraries in the examples; that is, code that comes as part of the Go installation. In real life, however, you'll use a mix of standard libraries and third-party code. Go's third-party ecosystem makes it very easy to run, in fact only a single command is required to get started with a third-party package hosted on the Internet using the go get tool. We'll be looking at how to consume third-party packages right now, but in a later chapter we'll also look at how we create and distribute our own.

 Source Control Software

Go can download third-party libraries stored in several varieties of source control software. If you attempt to download a package stored in source control software not on your system, you'll see a message along the lines of "go: missing Git command. See http://golang.org/s/gogetcmd." The vast majority of packages are stored in Git, so I suggest you install it if you're yet to do so. Visit http://golang.org/s/gogetcmd now and follow the link to install it. Go also supports Mercurial, Subversion, and Bazaar.

To see this in action, we're going to write a simple program that converts some markdown formatted text into HTML. If you've never heard of markdown, it's a way of writing formatted text in a simplified manner, and it's gaining popularity as a way to mark up text without having to know HTML.

We'll use a library called Black Friday by Russ Ross. The library is hosted on Github at github.com/russross/blackfriday. We tell Go to download the package first:

```
go get github.com/russross/blackfriday
```

This will download the library into your $GOPATH at $GOPATH/src/github.com/russross/blackfriday. If it runs correctly, there will be no output in the command line. If you run the command again it will be very fast, as Go knows you already have the package and don't need to download it again. To force an update, you can add the -u flag. Now you can simply import the library in your code and you're good to go. The library is referenced exactly as it was when we installed it: github.com/russross/blackfriday

markdown.go
```go
package main

import (
    "fmt"

    "github.com/russross/blackfriday"
)

func main() {
    markdown := []byte(`
# This is a header
* and
* this
* is
* a
* list
    `)
    html := blackfriday.MarkdownBasic(markdown)
    fmt.Println(string(html))
}
```

If you run this code, you'll see an output such as this:

```html
<h1>This is a header</h1>

<ul>
<li>and</li>
<li>this</li>
<li>is</li>
<li>a</li>
<li>list</li>
</ul>
```

There are a couple of points worth noting here. The first is that we're using backticks (`) to create a string that spans multiple lines, and we're also converting it to an array of bytes by surrounding it with parentheses preceded by a type []byte("some `string"`). We'll discuss byte arrays in a later chapter, but for the moment just think of them as another way to represent a string. Once we have our markdown ready, we create a new variable `html` that represents the HTML generated from the markdown. This is also a byte array, so when we print it out we first convert it back into a string `string(html)`.

You'll notice that we refer to the library as `blackfriday`, rather than the full path. The package name isn't defined by the URL, but by the `package xyz` command in the library's code; a general convention is that the last part of the path matches the name of the imported library.

 Go Getting Libraries

It's worth noting that the `go get` command doesn't just download the library that you've specified, it downloads all the other libraries used by the library you're downloading. As such, it's not uncommon to see multiple projects appear in your `$GOPATH` even though you've only asked for one library. You can use this to your advantage too: if we'd forgotten to run `go get github.com/russross/black-friday`, our code would have failed to compile, but we can run `go get` without any other parameters from inside the directory of our code, and Go would download all the dependencies for you. If you want to try this out, you can delete the `$GOPATH/src/github.com/russross/blackfriday` directory and run `go get` from the directory with the example code above.

Syntax Options and Conventions

Go is quite opinionated when it comes to how you should write your code; in fact, it has some very firm rules in place for this. Some formatting is enforced by the compiler, while some is convention.

Alternative Syntax Options

We'll look at a few syntax options here, namely ones that you might want to use in day-to-day programming, or come across in libraries you use.

Initializing Structs without Field Names

You can initialize struct types without specifying the field names. To do this, you have to pass in all the fields in the same order in which they're defined in the type definition; otherwise, you'll receive an error when compiling. Use this method where you can fit the values on one line and the number of fields in the struct are unlikely to change:

```
type Human struct {
    Name string
    Age  int
}
```

```
// Valid initialisation
me := Human{"Mal Curtis", 29}

// Error: cannot use 29 (type int) as type string in field value
// Error: cannot use "Mal Curtis" (type string) as type int in
// field value
me = Human{29, "Mal Curtis"}

// Error: too few values in struct initializer
me = Human{"Mal Curtis"}

// Error: mixture of field:value and value initializers
me = Human{"Mal Curtis", Age: 29}
```

Empty Variable Initialization

So far we've only been initializing variables by assigning them with :=. You can also explicitly declare a variable without assigning a value to it by using the var keyword followed by the variable name and its type:

```
var myString string // myString is an empty string
myString = "Hello!" // We don't need to use `:=` here
```

When initializing this way, the value assigned will be the "empty value" for the type. For number types this will be 0, and strings receive an empty string. Structs will be initialized, with all fields set to their empty values too. A pointer type will be set to nil, as will slices and maps:

```
var myMap map[string]string // myMap is nil
myMap["Test"] = "Hi" // panic: assignment to entry in nil map
```

You will still need to assign a map to the variable, but the variable's type will stay the same:

```
myMap = map[string]string{}
```

Trailing Commas

The last point to note on alternative syntaxes is that you can often rewrite comma-separated lists as multiple lines, but each line must have a trailing comma. Some languages or syntaxes do not allow a trailing comma, which makes rearranging the order of a list an annoying exercise. Go, however, not only allows a trailing comma, but requires it—if you leave it off your code won't compile. This applies only when writing on multiple lines. We've already seen this when initializing structs and maps, but it also works with slices:

```
mySlice := []string{"one", "two"} // Good

mySlice := []string{
    "one",
    "two",
} // Good

mySlice := []string{"one", "two",} // Compiler error

myMap := map[string]string{"one": "1", "two": "2"} // Good

myMap := map[string]string{
    "one": "1",
    "two": "2",
} // Good

myMap := map[string]string{
    "one": "1",
    "two": "2"
} // Bad
```

This also applies to defining and calling functions. You can list the parameters and return values on multiple lines if the definition becomes too long. The rule, as per usual, is that every line ending in a new line requires a comma:

```
// This is how we've seen functions so far.
func JoinTwoStrings(stringOne, stringTwo string) string {
    return stringOne + stringTwo
}
```

```
// This is also perfectly acceptable.
func JoinTwoStrings(
    stringOne,
    stringTwo string,
) string {
    return stringOne + stringTwo
}

// This is how we've seen calling functions so far.
myString := JoinTwoStrings("Hello", "World")

// This is also perfectly acceptable.
myString := JoinTwoStrings(
    "Hello",
    "World",
)
```

Coding Style Conventions

While it's not mandatory to follow these conventions, it makes sense to do so as they are used by both the standard library and most Go developers. Some of these conventions are controversial, such as using tabs for indenting, while others are fairly mundane, such as the choice for camel-casing variable names.

Here's a selection, by no means exhaustive, of the conventions that I believe you'll use in day-to-day programming.

Variable Naming

When naming variables, use camel case starting with a lowercase letter:

```
myVar := "something" // Good
variable := "something" // Good
MyVar := "something" // Bad
my_var := "something" // Bad
```

When using an abbreviation, stick to a consistent case depending on the initial character's case:

```
id := "123" // Good
myID := "123" // Good
Id := "123" // Bad
myId := "123" // Bad
```

Constants

In some languages it's common practice to capitalize constants; however, Go doesn't follow this convention, so just use camel case as we do for variables:

```
const retryTimeout = 60 // Good
const RETRY_TIMEOUT = 60 // Bad
const Retry_TIME_OUT = 60 // Worst
```

Constructors

The last aspect to note is the way that new instances of types are initialized. Rather than having the concept of a constructor as many languages do, the convention is to have a function that starts with new or New (depending on whether you want to export or not), followed by the type. This function would generally take whatever information is absolutely required for a working type as its parameters. For example, with our earlier Movie type, we may have a NewMovie(title string, year int) Movie function because we only need the title and year. Other values can be added later:

```
type Movie struct {
    Actors      []string
    Rating      float32
    ReleaseYear int
    Title       string
}

func NewMovie(title string, year int) Movie {
    return Movie{
        Title: title,
        ReleaseYear: year,
```

```
        Actors: []string{},
    }
}
```

Notice how we created an empty string array for the `Actors`? These new functions provide the opportunity to initialize empty structures that the type requires to function, and it's common practice to initialize empty arrays or maps within the new function.

Summary

If you've made it this far, you've pretty much covered the entire fundamentals of how to write Go programs! In the next chapter, we're going to have a look at some web development-specific coding. We'll also cover how to handle HTTP requests and responses, how Go handles templates, and how to write and read JSON.

Chapter 3

HTTP

Sending and receiving HTTP requests is at the core of every web application. Go's standard library contains a variety of packages that make this easy for us to do. In this chapter, we'll discover how we can respond to requests, route requests through middleware, create HTML templates, and create JSON responses—all with the standard Go library.

Responding to Requests

Creating a web server in Go is simple. In most languages, another piece of software is required for your application to be up and running on the Web, such as Apache for a PHP application. Go's standard library contains a package called `http`, which is powerful enough to run a server without using third-party software.

While there are a few ways to do it, the quickest way is to register a function to be run when a request is made whose URL matches a pattern. The function must have the signature `func(w http.ResponseWriter, r *http.Request)`. After we've registered a function to run, we start the server with `http.ListenAndServe`:

```
                                              1-hello-world/hello.go
package main

import (
    "fmt"
    "net/http"
)

func main() {
    http.HandleFunc("/", func(w http.ResponseWriter, r *http.
➥Request) {
        fmt.Fprintf(w, "Hello Gopher")
    })

    http.ListenAndServe(":3000", nil)
}
```

In this example, we've registered a function to run when a request is made to any path on port 3000. When run, the function uses `fmt.Fprintf` to write the string "`Hello Gopher`" to the response writer.

 Pattern Matching

The pattern "/" matches all requests. Pattern matching needs a little more explanation, so we'll cover it in depth later in the chapter.

You can see it in action by building and running your code, then visiting `http://127.0.0.1:3000` in your browser, which will look like Figure 3.1.

Figure 3.1. HTTP Hello World

Breaking It Down

The two parameters sent to the handler function provide all the functionality you need to respond to any type of request.

The first parameter is an instance of `http.ResponseWriter`, and we use it to write information that will be sent back to the browser. The response primarily consists of the body of a page, but also provides access to other information such as the headers or status code.

 Browsers Defined

I use the term "browser" loosely here as this applies to any method of sending requests, such as the command line tool cURL.

If you have cURL installed, you can run `curl -i 127.0.0.1:3000` instead of visiting via a browser.

The second parameter is an instance of `http.Request` and contains all the information we'd expect to see about a request, including any form data, query string values, and headers.

Adding More Information

There's little information in the response at the moment. In fact, the raw HTTP response is tiny:

```
HTTP/1.1 200 OK
Date: Mon, 01 Jun 2015 08:03:30 GMT
Content-Length: 12
Content-Type: text/plain; charset=utf-8

Hello Gopher
```

The first line lets us know we've received an `OK` HTTP response. This is followed by a few headers, the date, and content information. Note that the `Content-Type` is `text/plain`. Go will read the first 512 bytes of our response body and try to sniff out what type of response it is. Since there is no obvious type, it's given it a basic text type. The rest of the response makes up the body.

To provide more information, we need to manipulate the `ResponseWriter` object that is sent to our handler. The headers are represented by a `Header` map that you access via the appropriately named method `Header`. You can add a header via the `Add` method:

2-extra-headers/main.go *(excerpt)*

```
w.Header().Add("Server", "Go Server")
```

Adding a starting HTML tag will also trigger the content type sniffing to return a content type of `text/html`:

2-extra-headers/main.go *(excerpt)*

```
fmt.Fprintf(w, `<html>
    <body>
        Hello Gopher
    </body>
</html>`)
```

Run your server and you can see the new `Server` header and updated `Content-Type`:

```
HTTP/1.1 200 OK
Server: Go Server
Date: Mon, 01 Jun 2015 09:12:32 GMT
Content-Length: 57
Content-Type: text/html; charset=utf-8

<html>
    <body>
        Hello Gopher
    </body>
</html
```

Pattern Matching in Depth

Since all requests to a port are handled by by `http.ListenAndServe`, we need to have a way of routing requests for different resources to different parts of our code. Luckily, Go has a built-in way of doing this via the `http.ServeMux` type. `ServeMux` is a request multiplexer, which handles matching an incoming request's URL against the registered handlers and calling the handler for the pattern that most closely matches the URL. The `http` package creates a default `ServeMux` instance for you, and the `http.HandleFunc` function is actually a shortcut to the `(*ServeMux)` `HandleFunc` method on that default `ServeMux`.

When you create a `ServeMux`, you can then register different path patterns for it to match, along with a handler to run on those matches. Patterns don't have to match the path perfectly. There are two types of patterns: a path and a subtree. A **path** is defined without a trailing backslash (`/`), and refers to an explicit path. **Subtrees** are designed to match the start of a path, and include the trailing `/`, so if you request `/articles/latest` in our next example, you will see "`Hello from /articles/`" because `/articles/latest` matches `/articles/`. However, if you request `/users/latest` you will receive a 404, because the pattern `/users` lacks a trailing slash:

```
function main() {
    mux := http.ServeMux{}
    mux.Handle("/articles/",  func(w http.ResponseWriter, r *http.
➥Request) {
        fmt.Fprintf(w, "Hello from /articles/")
    })
    mux.Handle("/users",  func(w http.ResponseWriter, r *http.
➥Request) {
        fmt.Fprintf(w, "Hello from /users")
    })
    http.ListenAndServe(":3000", mux)
}
```

The length of a pattern is important too. The longer a pattern is, the higher a precedence it has. A pattern of `/articles/latest/` has a higher precedence than `/articles/`, for example. Because of this order precedence, it makes no difference which order you add the routes in. If we were to add in a handler for `/articles/latest/`, we could add it in either before or after the handler for `/articles/` and see absolutely no change in our code behavior:

```
func main() {
    mux := http.NewServeMux()
    mux.HandleFunc("/articles/",  func(w http.ResponseWriter,
➥r *http.Request) {
        fmt.Fprintf(w, "Hello from /articles/")
    })
```

```
    mux.HandleFunc("/articles/latest/",  func(w http.ResponseWriter,
➡r *http.Request) {
        fmt.Fprintf(w, "Hello from /articles/latest/")
    })
    mux.HandleFunc("/users",  func(w http.ResponseWriter, r *http.
➡Request) {
        fmt.Fprintf(w, "Hello from /users")
    })
    http.ListenAndServe(":3000", mux)
}
```

Hostname Matching

Patterns can also begin with a hostname, where only URLs for that hostname will match. A hostname match has a higher precedence than a pattern without a hostname.

Returning Errors

Sometimes things don't go as well as we'd like them to, and an error response is required—or at least a different response to 200 OK. Status codes are a hugely important part of the Web; without them we'd be unable to say when a resource isn't found; or when a page has moved; or when we're experiencing a problem and you should try back later.

A few of the more common status codes are:

- 301 Moved Permanently—used to redirect to another page
- 404 Not Found—when the requested resource doesn't exist
- 500 Internal Server Error—when an unexpected error occurs

The http package provides a function Error that takes the ResponseWriter, a message string, and the HTTP status code as an integer. For example, a 500 HTTP response is created like this:

```
http.HandleFunc("/", func(w http.ResponseWriter, r *http.Request) {
    http.Error(w, "Something has gone wrong", 500)
})
```

Every status code has semantic meaning so you should always endeavour to use the most appropriate one. If in doubt, remember that there are probably countless others before you who have tried to figure it out, and Google is your friend. For a full list of status codes, check out this Wikipedia article.[1]

Status Code Constants

The Go http package[2] includes a variety of constants that represent HTTP status codes. You can use these instead of normal integers as a way to have more declarative code. `http.StatusBadRequest` is a lot easier to understand than 400 for example.

Helper functions are provided for a couple of common use cases:

http.NotFound Probably one of the most common error responses is the 404 `Not Found`. The `http.NotFound` function takes both the `ResponseWriter` and `Request` instances.

http.Redirect This takes the `ResponseWriter`, `Request`, the URL to be redirected to (as a string), and the status code as an integer. There are several types of redirect status codes. The most common are 301 for permanently moved resources and 302 for temporarily moved resources.

---

[1] http://en.wikipedia.org/wiki/List_of_HTTP_status_codes
[2] http://golang.org/pkg/net/http/#pkg-constants

```
// Return a 404 Not Found
http.NotFound(w, req)

// Return a 301 Permanently Moved
http.Redirect(w, req, "http://anothersite.com", 301)
```

The Handler Interface

There is another way to register code to handle an HTTP request. Any type that implements the interface `http.Handler` can be passed to the `http.Handle` function, along with a pattern string. Just like we saw earlier with the `HandleFunc` function, this is a shortcut to the default `ServeMux` instance.

The `http.Handler` interface requires a single function, which has a signature matching that of the function sent to `http.HandleFunc`:

```
type Handler interface {
    ServeHTTP(ResponseWriter, *Request)
}
```

We can add a `ServeHTTP` function to almost any type we like. If we wanted to create a handler that returned the current uptime of the server in the response, we could create a new type `UptimeHandler`, and implement the `ServeHTTP` function:

```
                                                    3-time-handler/main.go
package main

import (
    "fmt"
    "net/http"
    "time"
)

// UptimeHandler writes the number of seconds since starting the
➥response
type UptimeHandler struct {
    Started time.Time
}

func NewUptimeHandler() UptimeHandler {
```

```
        return UptimeHandler{ Started: time.Now() }
}

func (h UptimeHandler) ServeHTTP(w http.ResponseWriter, req *http.
↪Request) {
    fmt.Fprintf(
        w,
        fmt.Sprintf("Current Uptime: %s", time.Since(h.Started)),
    )
}

func main() {
    http.Handle("/", NewUptimeHandler())
    http.ListenAndServe(":3000", nil)
}
```

When you run this and visit `http://127.0.0.1:3000` with your browser, you see the current uptime. The `time.Since` function returns a `time.Duration` object, representing the time lapsed since the server was started. The `time.Duration` type handles being converted to a string well and will display a human readable representation; for example, "Current Uptime: 4m20.843867792s".

Chaining Handlers to Create Middleware

In web development, the term **middleware** refers to a chain of handlers that wraps around your web app, adding extra functionality. It's a common concept that's often overlooked, and is very powerful when used correctly. Middleware can be used to authenticate users, compress response content, rate limit requests, capture application exceptions, and much more.

It's easy—and very common—to chain `http.Handlers` together to create middleware. For example, we could create a handler that requires a secret token to be sent via the query string in the request. If it finds the token, it will call the next handler; otherwise it will return a `404 Not Found` response:

```
// SecretTokenHandler secures a request with a secret token.
type SecretTokenHandler struct {
    next http.Handler
    secret string
}
```

```
// ServeHTTP makes SecretTokenHandler implement the http.Handler
➡interface.
func (h SecretTokenHandler) ServeHTTP(w ResponseWriter, req *
➡Request) {
    // Check the query string for the secret token
    if req.URL.Query().Get("secret_token") == h.secret {
        // The secret token matched, call the next handler
        h.next.ServeHTTP(w, req)
    }else{
        // No match, return a 404 Not Found response
        http.NotFound(w, req)
    }
}

func main() {
    http.Handle("/", SecretTokenHandler{
        next: NewUptimeHandler(),
        secret: "MySecret",
    })

    http.ListenAndServe(":3000", nil)
}
```

Attempting to request this page without the secret code will return a 404 `Not` `Found` response:

```
curl -i 127.0.0.1:3000
```

```
HTTP/1.1 404 Not Found
Content-Type: text/plain; charset=utf-8
Date: Mon, 01 Jun 2015 02:07:59 GMT
Content-Length: 19

404 page not found
```

But if you make the request with the secret token, you'll get the response from the next HTTP handler:

```
curl -i 127.0.0.1:3000/?secret_token=MySecret
```

```
HTTP/1.1 200 OK
Date: Mon, 01 Jun 2015 02:09:49 GMT
Content-Length: 31
Content-Type: text/plain; charset=utf-8

Current Uptime: 2m16.570254662s
```

HTML Templates

So far the examples we've looked at have been trivial, designed to examine a few specific use cases. What if we wanted to start returning responses that are a little more complicated? HTML would be difficult to generate if we had to use the simple `fmt` string functions to generate it.

Luckily Go provides its own HTML template package, `html/template`. This package not only allows us to easily format HTML pages from Go data types, but also handles the correct escaping of data into HTML output. For the most part, there will be no need to worry about escaping the data you pass into a template, as Go will manage this for you.

 Escaping

Escaping input on an HTML page is extremely important for both layout and security reasons. **Escaping** is the process of turning characters that have special meaning in HTML into HTML entities. For example, an ampersand is used to start an HTML entity, so if you wanted to display an ampersand correctly, you would have to write the HTML entity for one instead: `&amp;`. If you don't escape any data you try to display in your templates, then at best you might allow people to accidentally break your page layout, and at worst you open up your pages to malicious attackers.

If, for example, you have a blog featuring technical articles, you wouldn't want a post that had the content `</body>` to create an end body tag. Instead, you'd want it to display as text, which means converting it to the HTML `&lt;/body&gt;`. If you had comments on your blog, you'd want to avoid users being able to create comments with `<script>` tags that run JavaScript on your users' computers when they visit your page. This sort of security vulnerability is commonly referred to

> as **cross-site scripting**, or **XSS**. You can read much more on the topic at the Open Web Application Security Project (OWASP) website.[3]

The `html/template` package works in two steps. First you need to parse the HTML template into a `Template` type. After that, you can execute a data structure against that template to create your final output HTML.

Templates are created from plain strings, whether that's loaded in from a file or written directly in your Go code. Variable replacements, and control structures, are referred to as **actions** and are surrounded by "{{" and "}}" characters. Any text outside of an action is not modified.

A simple template that outputs "<h1> Hello World </h1>" would look like this:

```
                                              5-html-templates/main.go (excerpt)

package main

import (
    "html/template"
    "os"
)

func main() {
    tmpl, err := template.New("Foo").Parse("<h1>Hello {{.}}</h1>\n")
    if err != nil { panic(err) }
    err = tmpl.Execute(os.Stdout, "World")
    if err != nil { panic(err) }
}
```

Each template you create needs to be named. The reason for this will be covered later, so for the moment we'll just name each one "Foo".

The dot character that we see in `{{.}}` is known as the **dot action**, and refers to the data being passed into the template. Since we're just passing in a string, all we need to do is refer directly to the data, but dot can be assigned different data at different times; for example, when looping through data, dot is assigned the value of the current iteration. We'll see dot used again and again as we look at the different actions available to us in the template package.

---

[3] https://www.owasp.org/index.php/Cross-site_Scripting_(XSS)

Accessing Data

Accessing more complex data types is relatively simple in a template. While the method for accessing a struct field, map key, or simple function are different in Go, in the templates they look very similar. If we were executing the template against a struct, we could access any of its exported fields via their name. This example would print: "The Go html/template package" by Mal Curtis:

5-html-templates/main.go (excerpt)

```go
type Article struct{
    Name string
    AuthorName string
}

func main(){
    goArticle := Article{
        Name: "The Go html/template package",
        AuthorName: "Mal Curtis",
    }
    tmpl, err := template.New("Foo").Parse("'{{.Name}}' by
➥{{.AuthorName}}")
    if err != nil { panic(err) }
    err = tmpl.Execute(os.Stdout, goArticle)
    if err != nil { panic(err) }
}
```

The same applies for a map, simply refer to the key. Unlike field names, the key does not need to start with an uppercase character:

5-html-templates/main.go (excerpt)

```go
func main(){
    article := map[string]string{
        "Name": "The Go html/template package",
        "AuthorName": "Mal Curtis",
    }
    tmpl, err := template.New("Foo").Parse("'{{.Name}}' by
➥{{.AuthorName}}")
    if err != nil { panic(err) }
```

```
    err = tmpl.Execute(os.Stdout, article)
    if err != nil { panic(err) }
}
```

A function or method that takes no arguments can also be called in the same manner (referred to as a **niladic** function in the Go documentation). This example would output "`Written by Mal Curtis`":

5-html-templates/main.go (excerpt)

```
type Article struct{
    Name string
    AuthorName string
}

func(a Article) Byline() string{
    return fmt.Sprintf("Written by %s", a.AuthorName)
}

func main() {
    goArticle := Article{
        Name: "The Go html/template package",
        AuthorName: "Mal Curtis",
    }
    tmpl, err := template.New("Foo").Parse("{{.Byline}}")
    if err != nil { panic(err) }
    err = tmpl.Execute(os.Stdout, goArticle)
    if err != nil { panic(err) }
}
```

Conditionals with `if` and `else`

Now that we've seen how we can access data from various data structures, let's look at how we can control the flow of the template through conditional structures and loops.

Just like in our Go code, we have access to conditional flow through the use of `If` and `Else` statements. Nothing too difficult here—it will make up the bulk of the limited logic that templates have. Since we're unable to use parenthesis to specify what belongs inside the `if` statement, we use an **end** statement to signify the end boundary. This example appends the word "Draft" to a title if the article is yet to be published:

```
                                    5-html-templates/main.go (excerpt)

type Article struct{
    Name string
    AuthorName string
    Draft bool
}
func main(){
    goArticle := Article{
        Name: "The Go html/template package",
        AuthorName: "Mal Curtis",
    }
    tmpl, err := template.New("Foo").Parse(
        "{{.Name}}{{if .Draft}} (Draft){{end}}",
    )
    if err != nil { panic(err) }
    err = tmpl.Execute(os.Stdout, goArticle)
    if err != nil { panic(err) }
}
```

You can also specify an alternate template to display using an {{else}} block; for
example, {{if .Draft}} (Draft){{else}} (Published){{end}}.

Loops with Range

If you want to loop over a slice or map, you can do this with the range action. The
range action also has access to an optional {{else}} block, which is very useful
when it comes to listing a message when no items are available to loop over. Within
each loop, dot is set to the value being looped over. If you were to call the dot action
{{.}} inside a loop, it would be set to a different value in each iteration of the loop.
In this example, we would either get a list of article names and authors, or a message
saying "No published articles yet":

```
                                    5-html-templates/main.go (excerpt)

func main(){
    tmpl, err := template.New("Foo").Parse(`
    {{range .}}
        <p>{{.Name}} by {{.AuthorName}}</p>
    {{else}}
        <p>No published articles yet</p>
    {{end}}
    `)
```

```
    if err != nil { panic(err) }
    err = tmpl.Execute(os.Stdout, []Article{})
    if err != nil { panic(err) }
}
```

Multiple Templates

When you're parsing a template, you can actually define more than one template at a time. When it comes to running the code, you can decide which template to run, or even call a template from within another template. This allows for powerful templating, and encourages the reuse of template code—commonly referred to as creating **partials**.

You create a named template by using the {{define "FOO"}} action in your template input. This needs to be a top-level action; in other words, not part of any other action.

Adding Templates

You don't need to add all your templates in the one call to Parse. You can call Parse multiple times, or by using the ParseFiles and ParseGlob methods to load templates from file. We'll look at what a "Glob" is in a later chapter.

To call a template, you can either call ExecuteTemplate(wr io.Writer, name string, data interface{}) instead of the Execute method we've been using so far in our examples, or use the action {{template "FOO" context}}, where context is either dot or another value from the current context. The template action can also be called from inside another template, which is the key to template reuse.

For example, in our previous loop of articles, as the template for each article starts to grow it becomes harder to understand. You lose the ability to easily figure out the flow of the template, since it's not immediately obvious *where* you are. We could split the article template out from the template that loops it:

5-html-templates/main.go *(excerpt)*

```
func main(){
    tmpl, err := template.New("Foo").Parse(`
    {{define "ArticleResource"}}
        <p>{{.Name}} by {{.AuthorName}}</p>
    {{end}}
```

```
{{define "ArticleLoop"}}
    {{range .}}
        {{template "ArticleResource" .}}
    {{else}}
        <p>No published articles yet</p>
    {{end}}
{{end}}

{{template "ArticleLoop" .}}
`)
if err != nil { panic(err) }
err = tmpl.Execute(os.Stdout, []Article{})
if err != nil { panic(err) }
}
```

Now we can grow the size of the ArticleResource template without having to worry about the readability of the ArticleLoop template. We could also use the ArticleResource template from another completely separate template.

Pipelines

So far we've only seen simple access to data in our templates, but when it comes to real-world code, the data that a template receives is often not quite right for display. As an example, if we were outputting a price to the page, we'd probably want to format it with some currency information (such as a $), and perhaps limit it to two decimal places. Pipelines allow us to do this.

Pipelines are a way to evaluate data through a chain of commands. We've actually seen pipelines in action, we've just been using a single command, though—the dot is an example of a very simple pipeline with just one command.

Pipelines are chained by separating commands with the pipeline character (|). A command can either be a value, such as the dot value, or a function/method call where the arguments are separated by spaces, instead of parenthesis and commas such as printf format_string input_value.

The result of each command is piped into the next command as the last argument, which enables many commands to be piped together. The output of the last command becomes the value of the whole pipeline. Each command must output a single value, and an optional error as the second value. If there's an error, the template stops running and the error is returned as the response of the `Execute` function.

Go provides a few built-in functions that can be called. You can also provide your own functions to run. The built-in functions are a mixture of comparison, escaping, and printing helpers. We'll just look at one for the moment, but you can view the full list on the Go website.[4]

If we wanted to format a `float64` value as a currency, we could pass it through the `printf` function, which is an alias for the `fmt.Sprintf` function. In this example, we format the value `12.3` as a float with two decimal places, and the output would be "`Price: $12.30`":

5-html-templates/main.go (excerpt)

```go
func main(){
    tmpl, _ := template.New("Foo").Parse(
        "Price: ${{printf \"%.2f\" .}}\n",
    )
    tmpl.Execute(os.Stdout, 12.3)
}
```

We can rewrite this as a chain of commands by piping the dot to the `printf` function (remember, the value from one command is piped as the last argument to the next):

```go
func main(){
    tmpl, _ := template.New("Foo").Parse(
        "Price: ${{. | printf \"%.2f\"}}\n",
    )
    tmpl.Execute(os.Stdout, 12.3)
}
```

This makes more sense if we expand out our example to make the first value more complex, say, with a product that has a price and a quantity. If we want to display the total price for a product, we need to multiply the price by the quantity first. To do this, we require a function that is yet to exist.

We're able to easily register functions to use with our template. Any function we pass to the template has to follow the rules we saw earlier: one value returned and

---

[4] http://golang.org/pkg/text%2Ftemplate/#hdr-Functions

an optional second error value. Let's write a function called `Multiply` that takes two floats and returns their multiplied value:

```
// Multiply takes two float arguments and returns their multiplied
➥value
func Multiply(a, b float64) float64 {
    return a * b
}
```

Once we have the function, we register it with our template. We do this using the `Funcs` method, which takes a `FuncMap` value. A `FuncMap` is a map that has the function name used in the template as the key, and the function to run as the value:

```
map := template.FuncMap{
    "multiply": Multiply,
}
```

When we create our template, we break it into a few steps. We create the empty template, assign the `FuncMap`, then parse the template. If we try to parse the template before assigning the new function, it will throw an error, because it has no idea about the multiply function. Here we can see the result of the `multiply` function being passed to the `printf` function—outputting "Price: $24.60":

5-html-templates/main.go (excerpt)

```
type Product struct {
        Price    float64
        Quantity float64
}

func main() {
    tmpl := template.New("Foo")
    tmpl.Funcs(template.FuncMap{ "multiply": Multiply })

    tmpl, err := tmpl.Parse(
        "Price: ${{ multiply .Price .Quantity | printf \"%.2f\"}}
➥\n",
    )
    if err != nil { panic(err)  }

    err = tmpl.Execute(os.Stdout, Product{
        Price:    12.3,
```

```
            Quantity: 2,
    })
    if err != nil { panic(err)  }
}
```

And there we have it, we've added our own custom function and run it from our template! With the use of chained commands we're able to easily manipulate data into the correct format for display, right from our templates.

Here it is all together as one chunk of code:

```
package main

import (
    "os"
    "text/template"
)

type Product struct {
        Price     float64
        Quantity float64
}

func Multiply(a, b float64) float64 {
    return a * b
}

func main() {
    tmpl := template.New("Foo")
    tmpl.Funcs(template.FuncMap{ "multiply": Multiply })

    tmpl, err := tmpl.Parse(
        "Price: ${{ multiply .Price .Quantity | printf \"%.2f\"}}
➡\n",
    )
    if err != nil { panic(err)  }

    err = tmpl.Execute(os.Stdout, Product{
        Price:     12.3,
        Quantity: 2,
```

```
    })
    if err != nil { panic(err)  }
}
```

Variables

While not as important as some of the earlier concepts, you should note than you
don't have to access values from the data passed into a template each time. You are
able to set and use variables within your templates. A good example of why you
might want to do this would be if you were formatting a value the same way in
multiple places. It's easier and faster to just put the formatted value in a variable
and output it in multiple places.

Variables are set to the result of a pipeline, and look slightly different from normal
Go variables in that they must start with a dollar sign ($). We can rewrite the previous
example's template to use a variable this way:

5-html-templates/main.go *(excerpt)*

```
{{$total := multiply .Price .Quantity}}
Price: ${{ printf "%.2f" $total}}
```

 Variable Scope

A variable is limited to the scope that it was defined in. If you create it inside an
`if` or `range`, it will be unavailable outside that scope.

Rendering JSON

JSON, or **JavaScript Object Notation**, is a very common data format. While XML
used to be the *de facto* format employed to communicate between web systems, the
last five years have seen JSON replace it. If you're exposing your data to the Internet
these days, JSON is the format to expose it in. If you're unfamiliar with JSON, I recommend taking a look at the JSON Wikipedia article.[5]

JSON in Go is both written (marshaled) and read (unmarshaled) with the `encod-
ing/json` package.

---

[5] http://en.wikipedia.org/wiki/JSON#Data_types.2C_syntax_and_example

Marshaling

The process of converting a data type into JSON is known as marshaling the data. The JSON package is written to handle marshaling Go types into JSON without the need for a lot of boilerplate code. When you pass a type to be marshaled, Go does its best to figure out what it should look like as JSON.

 The Concept of "Marshaling"

Marshaling is used commonly in computer science to represent turning an object into a format that can be used to store or send the data to another system. It is similar to the term "serialising" and when referring to JSON you could use either; however, the Go authors have chosen to refer to it as "marshaling." The reverse is known as "unmarshaling" or "deserialising."

The main function used to marshal an object is `json.Marshal(interface{})` `([]byte, error)`. This function accepts any type, represented by the empty interface that all types satisfy. In return, you get a byte slice and an error if Go was unable to marshal the object.

 Byte Arrays

Byte arrays and slices are easily converted to strings with the `string` function, since a string is essentially a slice of bytes. This is a bit of an oversimplification, so if you'd like to understand more about how strings work in Go, check out this excellent post on the Go blog.[6]

Go will attempt to marshal the value by checking what type the value is. Strings are marshaled to JSON strings, Booleans are marshaled to JSON Booleans, and all number types encode to JSON numbers. If Go is able to traverse the value's fields (for a struct) or loop the value (such as with a map or slice), it will do so, attempting to marshal each item.

Marshaling Structs

Let's continue with our `Article` type used in the earlier examples:

---

[6] http://blog.golang.org/strings

```go
package main
type Article struct {
    Name string
    AuthorName string
    draft bool
}
func main(){
    article := Article{
        Name:       "JSON in Go",
        AuthorName: "Mal Curtis",
        draft:      true,
    }
    data, err := json.Marshal(article)
    if err != nil {
        fmt.Println("Couldn't marshal article:", err)
    }else{
        fmt.Println(string(data))
    }
}
```

If you run this, you'll see the following JSON:

```
{"Name":"JSON in Go","AuthorName":"Mal Curtis"}
```

You'll notice that the Name and AuthorName fields are there, but the draft field is missing. This is because Go will only convert exported fields in a struct. This makes sense, since an unexpected field is supposed to be private information, relevant only to the implementation of the type rather than externally exposed information.

You've probably also noticed that it's crudely formatted too. You can output an indented JSON representation by using the MarshalIndent function instead. With MarshalIndent, we supply a string prefix and indentation. Generally the prefix isn't used, but the indentation string is to pad out each level of indentation. The most common JSON indentation is two spaces, but you could use four, or a tab, or the emoji symbol for a cat—but other software might not be able to read it:

```go
data, _ := json.MarshalIndent(article, "", "  ")
fmt.Println(string(data))
```

Outputs:

```
{ "Name": "JSON in Go", "AuthorName": "Mal Curtis" }
```

Custom JSON Keys

If you've used JSON before, you might have seen that often the keys use underscore formatting, where instead of `AuthorName` it would be `author_name`. While there's no hard and fast rule you have to follow, sticking with conventions can make your data easier to consume. Luckily, we can easily change what our JSON looks like without affecting the Go structure, using a language feature called "tags".

Tags are added to the end of a field definition in a struct. They follow the format `type:"comma,separated,metadata"`. For JSON, we can specify some information with tags. We can change the key for a field, choose to completely exclude a field, or omit it if its value is empty:

```
type Product{
    // Field appears in JSON with the key "name".
    Name string `json:"name"`

    // Field appears in the JSON with the key "author_name",
    // but doesn't appear at all if its value is empty.
    AuthorName string `json:"author_name,omitempty"`

    // Field will not appear in the JSON representation.
    CommissionPrice float64 `json:"-"`
}
```

Nested Types

Since Go traverses the entire value when encoding it, it's easy to build up complex JSON structures. If we want to return an object with some meta data about a collection of articles along with the articles themselves, we could define a new type like this:

```
                                         6-marshaling-json/main.go (excerpt)
package main
type Article struct {
    Name string
}
type ArticleCollection struct {
```

```
    Articles []Article `json:"articles"`
    Total    int       `json:"total"`
}
func main(){
    p1 := Article{ Name: "JSON in Go" }
    p2 := Article{ Name: "Marshaling is easy" }
    articles := []Article{p1, p2}
    collection := ArticleCollection{
        Articles: articles,
        Total: len(articles),
    }
    data, err := json.MarshalIndent(collection, "", "  ")
    if err != nil { panic(err) }
    fmt.Println(string(data))
}
```

This would output:

```
{
  "articles": [
    {
      "name": "JSON in Go"
    },
    {
      "name": "Marshaling is easy"
    }
  ],
  "total": 2
}
```

… and that's about as complicated as JSON encoding gets in Go!

Unmarshaling Types

Unmarshaling an object refers to converting JSON into a typed data structure—the reverse of marshaling. Go handles unmarshaling by asking you to create a blank object of a type, and then attempts to apply the JSON string to that object.

As an example, we might want to load some configuration data from a file into a special config struct. Go will do its best to convert the data into the appropriate format. Say that we had the following file saved as `config.json`:

```
{
    "SiteName": "My Cat Blog",
    "SiteUrl": "www.mycatblog.com",
    "Database": {
        "Name": "cats",
        "Host": "127.0.0.1",
        "Port": 3306,
        "Username": "user1",
        "Password": "Password1"
    }
}
```

We could create a matching data struct, then unmarshal the data into it with the
`json.Unmarshal` function. This function takes two parameters, the byte array of
JSON data, and the pointer to the object that should have the data applied to it:

7-unmarshaling-json/main.go *(excerpt)*

```
type Config struct {
    Name      string `json:"SiteName"`
    URL       string `json:"SiteUrl"`
    Database struct {
        Name      string
        Host      string
        Port      int
        Username string
        Password string
    }
}
conf := Config{}
data, err := iouitil.ReadData("config.json")
if err != nil { panic(err) }

err = json.Unmarshal(data, &conf)
if err != nil { panic(err) }

fmt.Printf("Site: %s (%s)", conf.Name, conf.URL)

db := conf.Database
// Print out a database connection string.
fmt.Printf(
    "DB: mysql://%s:%s@%s:%d/%s",
    db.Username,
    db.Password,
```

```
    db.Host,
    db.Port,
    db.Name,
)
```

In this example we'd see the following output:

```
Site: My Cat Blog (www.mycatblog.com)
DB: mysql://user1:Password1@127.0.0.1:3306/cats
```

Notice how the database port has been assigned to an `int` data type. Since Go has several `int` data types (`int`, `int32`, and `int64`), it's not picky about what you try to unmarshal a JSON number into, as long as it's of the same general type, such as an integer or float.

If you happen to have extra keys in your JSON not represented by a matching field in a struct, Go will quietly ignore them.

Unknown JSON Structure

Sometimes you might not know the exact format of the JSON that you need to unmarshal. In these cases, it can be tricky. It's recommended to first try ensuring that your data input fits a known format. If selecting a type for an unknown input, if you use the blank interface type `interface{}`, any input will be a valid type. The problem then becomes accessing the data, as you have to coerce the data back to a stricter type if you want to do anything useful with it.

As a quick example of loading unknown data, here's a function that prints the "foo" key from some JSON:

8-unknown-json-input *(excerpt)*

```
package main
func FooJSON(input string) {
    data := map[string]interface{}{}
    err := json.Unmarshal([]byte(input), &data)
    if err != nil { panic(err) }

    foo, _ := data["foo"]

    switch foo.(type) {
```

```go
    case float64:
        fmt.Printf("Float %f\n", foo)
    case string:
        fmt.Printf("String %s\n", foo)
    default:
        fmt.Printf("Something else\n")
    }
}

func main() {
    FooJSON(`{
        "foo": 123
    }`)
    FooJSON(`{
        "foo": "bar"
    }`)
    FooJSON(`{
        "foo": []
    }`)
}
```

This would output: `Float 123.000000 String bar Something else`

Note how the JSON input with the integer ended up with type `float64`. This is because JSON doesn't differentiate between integers and floats, it just has the type "number". Since Go is unable to infer the expected data type, it defaults to `float64`.

Summary

In this chapter, we had a look at how you can create a web server with Go, and how to chain functions to create middleware. We looked at the comprehensive `html/template` package to see how we manage our HTML templates, and saw how we can marshal and unmarshal the JSON format.

That's it for the HTTP package so far. We'll start putting the information that we've just learned to good use very soon.

Gophr Part 1: The Project

The next few chapters are dedicated to a real-life project. No more "Hello Worlds" here. We're going to build a real website, with real logic and real processes. After we're done, I'm trusting you'll have a solid understanding for why Go is such a great language, and feel equipped to start your own projects.

You have probably heard of the website Flickr[1], one of the earliest and most famous photo-sharing sites. Flickr allows you to upload, store, view, and share your photographs. What you may not have heard of, however, is Gophr. That's because we're yet to create it—but that's about to change! We're going to start building Gophr, our own photo-sharing service written in Go.

Unfortunately, we'll be unable to fit in all the features that Flickr has, so we'll limit ourselves to the basics. Anyone will be able to come along to Gophr, sign up for an account, and upload their images. Once uploaded, we'll handle storing and resizing images for display, and let people view them, too.

---

[1] http://www.flickr.com/

There are quite a few complex processes involved in these features, so we'll be tackling them one at a time. While we're building Gophr, we'll also explore some of the features of Go that I have yet to talk about—but more on that later.

This chapter is going to focus purely on the skeleton of our project. It will provide the bones that enables our application to hold itself together. None of the code we write in this chapter is specific to the Gophr site; it's all about providing a nice base that you could use for any web application. We'll deal with static assets, templates, layouts, advanced middleware, and advanced routing.

Using Bootstrap

Since we're focusing on the business logic rather than the design of our web service, I will be using Bootstrap to give us a base design and collection of UI components. **Bootstrap** is an assortment of stylesheets and JavaScript code that takes the hassle out of many common website design tasks. This way we'll be able to avoid dealing with what makes the service pretty, instead focusing on the nitty-gritty of building a secure, stable, and fast web service.

You'll find the Bootstrap source code in the code directory for this project, but feel free to head to the Bootstrap website for the latest version. As I write, the current version is 3.2.0, and the templates we write should be valid for any 3.x version of Bootstrap.

 Bootstrap

If you're unfamiliar with Bootstrap, I highly recommend heading to getbootstrap.com[2] and having a read. While not all projects will need it, Bootstrap is a great way to rapidly prototype a site. If you want to dive a little deeper, I suggest reading the SitePoint book *Jump Start Bootstrap*.[3]

Project Layout

Our first task is to figure out where all our files are going to live. We'll need a place not only for our Go code but also our assets, such as templates, CSS, and JavaScript. To do this, we'll lock away those files in directories inside an **assets** directory.

---

[2] http://getbootstrap.com/
[3] https://learnable.com/books/jump-start-bootstrap

Create a directory for your project, and then create directories that match the format here (don't worry about any of the files yet, it's just the directory structure we're interested in):

```
assets/
    js/
        app.js
        bootstrap.js
    css/
        app.css
        bootstrap.css
    fonts/
        bootstrap.ott
    images/
        logo.png
    data/
        # uploaded files will go in here
templates/
    users/
        new.html
        edit.html
main.go
handlers.go
user.go
image.go
etc…
```

Our Go files will live in the root directory, but our assets are nicely grouped away by their functionality (trust me, you want to avoid mixing up your JavaScript with your CSS and images). Note that the images directory is for the site images, rather than the user-uploaded images. At this point, you should also copy the Bootstrap files into their respective directories; the Bootstrap download contains directories that match the names we're using.

For templates, we'll stick to a naming convention of subdirectories for the "object" that we're dealing with, such as **users** or **images**, and files named for the `action` we're going to perform, such as **new** or **edit**. We'll also define templates by name inside each of those files, so `templates/users/new.html` would be expected to define the template `users/new` by using a define block like so:

```
{{define "users/new"}}
<!-- Content Here -->
{{end}}
```

Serving Assets

It'd be a real pain if we had to create routes for every asset we wanted to serve up, or write a handler to check the file system for files. Luckily the net/http library has a built-in file server for us to use! With a few lines of code, we're able to create a handler that will happily serve up our asset files. Even better, we can mount that route to only deal with requests to the path /assets/, ensuring that we're not serving up any source code or other irrelevant files.

To create a file server, you'll need to call the function FileServer(root FileSystem) Handler. As you can see, this takes a FileSystem object and returns an http.Handler. A FileSystem object represents a path on the host file system, and it's easy to create a FileSystem object using the Dir function. If we want a FileSystem object that represents our assets, we can just call http.Dir('/assets/') and pass that into the FileServer function. We can then use the returned handler in our app:

```
// Super Simple static webserver:
log.Fatal(http.ListenAndServe(":3000", http.FileServer(http.Dir
➥("assets/"))))
```

We don't want to serve up assets at the root of our website—we want them available at /assets/. We can easily add a ServeMux to handle requests to /assets/, but since the requested file would then include the /assets/ part, it would look in the file system for assets/assets/. To fix this, we pass our FileSystem object through the StripPrefix function, which allows us to strip the /assets/ from the request so that the correct files are served up:

```
// Simple static webserver:
mux := http.NewServeMux()
mux.Handle("/assets/", http.StripPrefix("/assets/", http.FileServer
```

```
➥(http.Dir("assets/"))))

log.Fatal(http.ListenAndServe(":3000", mux))
```

If you run this code and place a file into the assets directory, you'll be able to request the file via a URL:

```
echo "This is a static text file!" > assets/test.txt
curl -i 127.0.0.1:3000/assets/test.txt
```

```
HTTP/1.1 200 OK
Accept-Ranges: bytes
Content-Length: 28
Content-Type: text/plain; charset=utf-8
Last-Modified: Mon, 01 Jun 2015 09:36:07 GMT
Date: Mon, 01 Jun 2015 09:49:36 GMT

This is a static text file!
```

The cool thing to note here is that a `Last-Modified` header has been added. Go's `FileServer` is reading the metadata from the file and adding the header. If a request comes in with an `If-Modified-Since` header that is on or before this date, Go will return a `304 Not Modified` and no body content. This allows the browser to cache a file and only request files if they've been updated. Your browser will handle these headers, sending an `If-Modified-Since` date if it's seen the file before and received a `Last-Modified` header. If it receives a `304` response, it just serves up the file from its cache. Fewer data has to be transferred, and your application has to do less work.

 304 All the Things

Last-Modified headers aren't just for static files. If you design your service well, you can use the same process to say that data has yet to be updated since a given time. If a user has data that's still valid, you can return a 304 and the page doesn't have to be rerendered, the data won't need to be fetched from the database, and everything is superfast for the user:

```
GET /assets/test.txt HTTP/1.1
If-Modified-Since:Mon, 01 Jun 2015 09:50:11 GMT

HTTP/1.1 304 Not Modified
Date: Mon, 01 Jun 2015 09:53:56 GMT
```

Rendering Pages

If we had to manually load a template in every handler, we would quickly see our code grow bloated, repeating a lot of functionality unnecessarily. Instead, we can move the loading and rendering of templates into a single area. Since our templates are defined by name, it's easy enough to load all templates at once when we start our program. This way the work is done at initialization when you start the program, rather than in every request. It also means it will happen once, and only once.

Let's start by creating a few files. We'll need a **main.go** file to start our app and **template.go** to contain the logic for rendering our templates. Let's also create a template in **templates/index/home.html** to contain our home page logic.

We'll create a basic home page template with a link to register a Gophr account. We'll be making plenty of changes to this page throughout the project, so for the moment it's okay to keep it simple and assume people are without an account:

2_first_template/templates/index/home.html

```
{{define "index/home"}}
<html>
    <head>
        <link rel="stylesheet" href="/assets/css/bootstrap.css">
    </head>
    <body>
        <nav class="navbar navbar-default" role="navigation">
            <div class="container-fluid">
                <div class="navbar-header">
                    <a class="navbar-brand" href="/">Gophr</a>
                </div>
                <div class="collapse navbar-collapse">
                    <p class="navbar-text navbar-right">
                        <a href="/register" class="navbar-link">
➥Register</a>
```

```
                </p>
              </div>
            </div>
          </nav>
        </body>
      </html>
    {{end}}
```

The HTML is very basic, with just a stylesheet and a navigation bar. The HTML structure and class names are for a Bootstrap navigation bar, with the Gophr brand on the left, and a register link on the right. To serve up this template, we'll need to parse all our templates, then add a function to render a template to a response. All we require for this function is the `http.ResponseWriter` to render to, the name of the template, and any data that the template might require:

2_first_template/template.go *(excerpt)*

```
var templates = template.Must(template.New("t").ParseGlob("
➥templates/**/*.html"))
```

Our first piece of code is not inside a function so it will run immediately, and the result is stored inside a variable `templates`. We're creating a new template instance called `t`, and telling it to parse the files that match the glob `templates/**/*.html`. As we discussed earlier, this matches how we're planning on storing our templates.

Both **templates/index/home.html** and **templates/foo/bar/baz.html** will match the glob, but **templates/test.html** won't as the path needs at least one directory inside the `templates` directory.

 ## File System Globs

A **glob** is a way to find files that match a specific pattern. The `**/` part says to match at least one directory with any name, and the `*.html` part is to match any file ending in .html. Combined with the prefix "templates" this will match any files ending in **.html** that are at least one directory deep inside the templates directory.

Using `template.Must`

We've wrapped our template parsing code inside a call to `template.Must`. This function returns the template if it is valid; however, if an error is encountered when loading the files it will panic, and we'll see an immediate failure. We do this so that the app will fail to start, rather than waiting until the first request to see an error, or do additional error-checking outside the main function.

2_first_template/template.go (excerpt)

```go
func RenderTemplate(w http.ResponseWriter, r *http.Request, name
➥string, data interface{}) {
    err := templates.ExecuteTemplate(w, name, data)
    if err != nil {
        http.Error(
            w,
            fmt.Sprintf(errorTemplate, name, err),
            http.StatusInternalServerError,
        )
    }
}

var errorTemplate = `
<html>
    <body>
        <h1>Error rendering template %s</h1>
        <p>%s</p>
    </body>
</html>
`
```

Now we have a function to render a template to our `http.ResponseWriter`. The function `Template.ExecuteTemplate` takes an object that satisfies the `io.Writer` interface, the name of the template to execute, and any data that should be supplied. `http.ResponseWriter` satisfies the `io.Writer` interface, since it has a method `Write(p []byte) (n int, err error)`. We can happily pass along no data if required, but our templates will definitely be needing data at some point.

If an error is found when trying to render our template, we manually render a basic error page with some information about what happened, and what we were trying to do. By rendering out to the browser this way, you'll avoid having to jump back to the command line to figure out what went wrong, as it will be immediately apparent.

It's important to note that we accept data in the format `interface{}`. This is the "empty interface" type, which has no methods and therefore all types satisfy it. Since the template package handles information in a variety of ways, this is what it accepts so it's what we'll pass it.

Lastly, we need to wire it all together into a server that can handle requests. For the moment we'll wire up the root path, /, to render the home page template along with adding our **assets** file server. To render the home page, we'll just call `RenderTemplate` with the name of our template (`index/home`), and `nil` for the data:

```
                                      2_first_template/main.go (excerpt)
func main() {
    mux := http.NewServeMux()

    mux.HandleFunc("/", func(w http.ResponseWriter, r *http.
➡Request) {
        RenderTemplate(w, r, "index/home", nil)
    })

    mux.Handle(
        "/assets/",
        http.StripPrefix("/assets/", http.FileServer(http.Dir
➡("assets/"))),
    )

    http.ListenAndServe(":3000", mux)
}
```

Now if you compile and run your app, then visit `http://127.0.0.1:3000` in your browser, you'll be welcomed with the Gophr navigation bar as seen in Figure 4.1! Beautiful.

Figure 4.1. The home page viewed in Chrome on Windows

Creating a Layout

We're developers, and we love avoiding repetitive code, right? So before we jump in and start creating other pages, let's ensure that we're not writing out our entire HTML structure for every page's template.

Since all pages will have the same basic layout (or at the very least, most pages), we'll create a way to render our templates within the same layout on every page. All the HTML boilerplate required by every page can go into this layout, and we can keep our templates thin, with just the content that makes each page unique.

Go doesn't support layouts directly out of the box, so we'll need to write our own way of handling layouts. To do this we'll create a layout file. In this file, we'll write our layout HTML, and then add a function call {{ yield }} where we want our content to be rendered. We'll be creating the yield function ourselves, and while it has no special meaning in and of itself, it's a common term used in a variety of programming languages to defer control to other code, so it makes sense as a function name:

```
                                              3_layouts/templates/layout.html
<html>
    <head>
        <link rel="stylesheet" href="/assets/css/bootstrap.css">
    </head>
    <body>
    {{ yield }}
    </body>
</html>
```

Now that the layout HTML is in our layout file, we can remove it from our template:

```
                                    3_layouts/templates/index/home.html
{{define "index/home"}}
<nav class="navbar navbar-default" role="navigation">
    <div class="container-fluid">
        <div class="navbar-header">
            <a class="navbar-brand" href="/">Gophr</a>
        </div>
        <div class="collapse navbar-collapse">
            <p class="navbar-text navbar-right">
                <a href="/register" class="navbar-link">Register</a>
            </p>
        </div>
    </div>
</nav>
{{end}}
```

First up, we'll create a new template instance for our layout. Before we can load our layout file, we'll need to add in a funcMap with a `yield` function. If we try to load **layout.html** before we add a `yield` function, it will throw a bit of a tantrum. We'll create a default `yield` function that returns an error if it's called.

 Default Template Names

> Rather than executing named templates, we'll name this template `layout.html` the same as our actual layout file. This way we can just call `Execute` and it knows what template to run (templates loaded with `ParseFiles` are named after the file they are in by default).

```
                                          3_layouts/template.go (excerpt)
var layoutFuncs = template.FuncMap{
    "yield": func() (string, error) {
        return "", fmt.Errorf("yield called inappropriately")
    },
}
var layout = template.Must(
    template.
        New("layout.html").
```

```
        Funcs(layoutFuncs).
        ParseFiles("templates/layout.html"),
)
```

So now we have a layout variable that contains our layout template. When it comes to actually rendering the right content when we call `yield`, we create a new `yield` function with each request. Every time we run `RenderTemplate`, we change the `yield` function to render the named template with the supplied data, just like our original code. Instead of rendering to the `ResponseWriter`, though, we'll write to a buffer and return the rendered template as a string:

3_layouts/template.go (excerpt)

```
funcs := template.FuncMap{
    "yield": func() (template.HTML, error) {
        buf := bytes.NewBuffer(nil)
        err := templates.ExecuteTemplate(buf, name, data)
        return template.HTML(buf.String()), err
    },
}
```

Error Bubbling

If you remember back to Chapter 3, we learned that a custom function can return content and an optional error as the second parameter. We'll be returning an HTML template (our content) and an error (the error from rendering our content). This will pass any error rendering our content into the layout template, which in turn will return that error to the code that executes it.

This goes inside `RenderTemplate`. It defines a new funcMap that overwrites the `yield` function with one that renders the named template (such as `"index/home"`), and returns it along with any error that might have occurred. We return it as an instance of `template.html` so that the layout template file treats it as sanitised HTML—otherwise it would consider it unsafe and end up double encoding all the HTML in the template, which isn't at all what we want!

Next we'll update our layout to use the new function, then render the layout to the `ResponseWriter`. Now we could just update the `layout` variable with the new funcMap and execute it, but that might give us funny results at some point. If two requests were to come in at the same time, one might overwrite the funcMap in-between the other overwriting it and executing it. This could result in a page being rendered with the wrong template. To ensure this never happens, we first clone the layout variable, which gives us our own copy to play with completely separate of the shared layout variable:

3_layouts/template.go *(excerpt)*

```
    layoutClone, _ := layout.Clone()
    layoutClone.Funcs(funcs)
    err := layoutClone.Execute(w, data)
```

So we clone the layout to get our own variable that we can update willy-nilly without affecting other requests. We then set its funcMap to use our special `yield` function that will render the correct template with the supplied data. Finally, we execute our layout, which renders it to the `ResponseWriter`. There's no need to pass any data to this method, since it's supplied directly in the `yield` function.

Here's the finished product:

3_layouts/template.go *(excerpt)*

```
var layoutFuncs = template.FuncMap{
    "yield": func() (string, error) {
        return "", fmt.Errorf("yield called inappropriately")
    },
}
var layout = template.Must(
    template.
        New("layout.html").
        Funcs(layoutFuncs).
        ParseFiles("templates/layout.html"),
)

var templates = template.Must(template.New("t").ParseGlob("
➥templates/**/*.html"))

func RenderTemplate(w http.ResponseWriter, r *http.Request, name
➥string, data interface{}) {
    funcs := template.FuncMap{
        "yield": func() (template.HTML, error) {
            buf := bytes.NewBuffer(nil)
            err := templates.ExecuteTemplate(buf, name, data)
            return template.HTML(buf.String()), err
```

```
        },
    }

    layoutClone, _ := layout.Clone()
    layoutClone.Funcs(funcs)
    err := layoutClone.Execute(w, data)

    if err != nil {
        http.Error(
            w,
            fmt.Sprintf(errorTemplate, name, err),
            http.StatusInternalServerError,
        )
    }
}

var errorTemplate = `
<html>
    <body>
        <h1>Error rendering template %s</h1>
        <p>%s</p>
    </body>
</html>
`
```

Advanced Routing

The built-in `http.ServeMux` router is a great way to start handling requests in Go, but it lacks some of the more fine-grained controls that many web frameworks provide. For example, determining whether a request is a GET or a POST is left up to the handler itself. If you wanted to handle a GET request differently to a POST—which almost all of the time you will—you'd have to do a conditional check inside the handler for the request and perform different logic. While this is doable, it's not ideal, and we should be able to assign a handler for each HTTP verb.

 HTTP Verbs

An **HTTP verb** is used to describe the type of request that's being made. Most requests are GET requests, intended to get information rather than modify it. You'll probably know of POST requests, used when submitting a form, but you may not have heard of some of the other request types, such as PUT, DELETE, and HEAD requests. Each of these verbs have a different semantic meaning, used to describe what a request should be doing. A GET shouldn't modify data, while a POST is used to create a resource; PUT is used to update an existing resource, and DELETE is self-explanatory.

Another task that `http.ServeMux` handles below par is matching parameters in a URL. If we wanted to have a URL that described an image that belongs to a user, we might have this: `http://gophr.com/users/1234/images/5678`, where 1234 is the user ID, and 5678 is the image ID. To match this request, we'd use a pattern of `/users/`, and then check if the path format matched some numbers, followed by the string `/images/` and some more numbers. This would quickly become unruly. Just as with the GET versus POST handlers, we'd have to be performing logic inside our handlers, and lots of it.

Instead of using `http.ServeMux`, we require a router that's more powerful. There are plenty of good third-party routers available, but for Gophr we're going to use my favorite: the excellent `httprouter` package. This package provides us with all the conveniences that a modern router package should provide. We can assign handlers to only specific HTTP verbs, and we can add powerful pattern-matching to our routes, including named parameters. Named parameters allow us to capture part of a url into a named value that we can access in our requests. If we continue with our earlier example of accessing a user's image at `/users/1234/images/5678`, we can define a route of `/users/:user_id/images/:image_id` and then gain access to the actual values in our handler. There's no need to check the URL, as the router has done this for us.

 httprouter Version

Download httprouter via `go get github.com/julienschmidt/httprouter`.

The version of `httprouter` that I used was `afa7ae2`. If you're having trouble with the example code, the API might have changed. You can either use the same commit as I did, or check the documentation for the new API.

Using `httprouter`

httprouter is similar in many regards to the `http.ServeMux` we've used so far. In fact, we can still use any `http.Handler` or `http.HandleFunc` if we want to. If we were to do that, though, we'd fail to gain access to the named variables; we can use a new type, `httprouter.Handle` instead. The only aspect different to `http.Handler` is an added third parameter of type `httprouter.Params`, which is an array of key-value pairs for the named parameters in a request.

Handling our user's image request, we access the user ID and image ID, which would both be in the `params` array:

```
func HandleUserImage(w http.ResponseWriter, r *http.Request, params
➡Params){
    userID := params.ByName("user_id")
    imageID := params.ByName("image_id")
}
```

If we visited `/users/1234/images/5678`, `userID` and `imageID` would be equal to the strings "1234" and "5678" respectively. It's unnecessary to even look at the request URL; it's all packaged up for us in a neat little `params` array and passed into the function.

Flexible Middleware

Since we're going to be creating a complex application, we should invest a little time in making our middleware easy to use. Otherwise our application will turn into a bit of a mess, and we'll end up with a lot of duplicated code. We briefly touched on middleware in the last chapter, but didn't create a flexible middleware. Instead, we required each handler to be responsible for calling the next handler in the chain. You can think of this as the **onion model**, where each handler calls the next handler, ending up with handlers wrapped in handlers.

Instead of having the responsibility for calling the next handler inside any given handler, we can use the **chain model** . This moves the responsibility for calling the next handler up a layer, creating a chain of handlers that knows when a response has been written, and will stop processing when a handler writes a response. This means we can register as many handlers as we want, and each one will be processed until one chooses to write a response and break the chain.

To do this, we perform two tasks. First up we define a new type, which is an array of `http.Handlers`. By adding a `ServeHTTP` method to this type, we're able to make an array of handlers to satisfy the `Handler` interface—kind of like the movie *Inception*, it's handlers all the way down. We'll also write a function to add handlers to the middleware, which is a vanity helper that simply appends the handler to the array. We do this so that we avoid the end user knowing about the underlying type of `Middleware`:

```
4_http_router/middleware.go (excerpt)

type Middleware []http.Handler

// Adds a handler to the middleware
func (m *Middleware) Add(handler http.Handler) {
    *m = append(*m, handler)
}
func (m Middleware) ServeHTTP(w http.ResponseWriter, r *http.
➥Request) {
  // Process the middleware
}
```

The `ServeHTTP` method will loop through each of the handlers in the array, stopping only when a response is written. To figure out when a response is written, we add a second type into the mix. Earlier we saw that every `http.Handler` writes to a `http.ResponseWriter`. What you might have failed to notice is that `http.ResponseWriter` isn't a concrete implementation, but an interface instead. This means that we can create our own type that implements the `http.ResponseWriter` interface, and add further logic to the type that we'll use to know when a response has been written, and stop our middleware chain.

Let's take a look at what our middleware `ResponseWriter` looks like. We create a struct type, which includes an embedded `http.ResponseWriter` and a boolean field to let us know if we've written a response. You should add the code we're writing here to a file called **middleware.go** in the project root. We'll use this file to group our HTTP-related logic:

```
4_http_router/middleware.go (excerpt)

type MiddlewareResponseWriter struct {
    http.ResponseWriter
    written bool
}

func NewMiddlewareResponseWriter(w http.ResponseWriter) *
➥MiddlewareResponseWriter {
    return &MiddlewareResponseWriter{
```

```
        ResponseWriter: w,
    }
}
```

We've also added a function called `NewMiddlewareResponseWriter`, which takes a `http.ResponseWriter` and returns a `MiddlewareResponseWriter` that wraps it.

Since we're embedding the `http.ResponseWriter`, our type already satisfies the `http.ResponseWriter` interface but lacks the functionality we need. To do that we override the methods that write to the response. The methods we're interested in are `Write(bytes []byte) (int, error)` and `WriteHeader(code int)`. In both cases we want to receive these calls, mark the response as written, and then pass the arguments to the original `http.ResponseWriter`:

4_http_router/middleware.go (excerpt)

```
func (w *MiddlewareResponseWriter) Write(bytes []byte) (int,
➥error) {
    w.written = true
    return w.ResponseWriter.Write(bytes)
}

func (w *MiddlewareResponseWriter) WriteHeader(code int) {
    w.written = true
    w.ResponseWriter.WriteHeader(code)
}
```

So now if we pass an instance of `MiddlewareResponseWriter` to an `http.Handler` and the `http.Handler` calls `Write` or `WriteHeader`, we'll mark the response as written to and then defer to the original `Write` or `WriteHeader` method.

All that's left at this point is to write the `ServeHTTP` method for our middleware. That's the one that will get a standard `http.ResponseWriter`, wrap in our `MiddlewareResponseWriter`, and loop through the handlers until one is written. If no handler writes to the response, we'll write a `404 Not Found` response:

4_http_router/middleware.go (excerpt)

```
func (m Middleware) ServeHTTP(w http.ResponseWriter, r *http.
➥Request) {
    // Wrap the supplied ResponseWriter
```

```
mw := NewMiddlewareResponseWriter(w)

// Loop through all the registered handlers
for _, handler := range m {
    // Call the handler with our MiddlewareResponseWriter
    handler.ServeHTTP(mw, r)

    // If there was a write, stop processing
    if mw.written {
        return
    }
}
// If no handlers wrote to the response, it's a 404
http.NotFound(w, r)
}
```

 Reusable Packages

A lot of the code we've written so far would be useful as a package that you can use in multiple projects. Rather than attempting to do that now, and putting the cart before the horse, we'll look at how to do this after we've completed the whole Gophr project.

How Routing Works with Our Middleware

You might be thinking "How does routing work with our middleware?", and that's a good question. How *are* we going to route requests for all our pages to the correct handler? Well, for starters, we're going to have two separate routers: one for unauthenticated requests, such as signing up and viewing users and their images, and another router for authenticated requests, such as uploading and editing images. We'll be adding these routers to our middleware, but in between them we'll add an authentication handler that ensures the request is authenticated, and redirect the user to sign in if they're not signed in:

4_httprouter/main.go (excerpt)

```
func main() {
    unauthenticatedRouter := NewRouter()
    unauthenticatedRouter.GET("/", HandleHome)

    authenticatedRouter := NewRouter()
```

```
    authenticatedRouter.GET("/images/new", HandleImageNew)

    middleware := Middleware{}
    middleware.Add(unauthenticatedRouter)
    middleware.Add(http.HandlerFunc(AuthenticateRequest))
    middleware.Add(authenticatedRouter)

    http.ListenAndServe(":3000", middleware)
}
```

4_httprouter/auth.go (excerpt)

```
func AuthenticateRequest(w http.ResponseWriter, r *http.Request){
  // Redirect the user to login if they're not authenticated
    authenticated := false
    if !authenticated {
        http.Redirect(w, r, "/register", http.StatusFound)
    }
}
```

4_httprouter/handle_index.go (excerpt)

```
func HandleHome(w http.ResponseWriter, r *http.Request, params
➥httprouter.Params){
  // Display Home Page
    RenderTemplate(w, r, "index/home", nil)
}
```

4_httprouter/handle_user.go (excerpt)

```
func HandleUserNew(w http.ResponseWriter, r *http.Request, params
➥httprouter.Params) {
    // Display Home Page
    RenderTemplate(w, r, "users/new", nil)
}
```

4_httprouter/handle_image.go (excerpt)

```
func HandleImageNew(w http.ResponseWriter, r *http.Request, params
➥httprouter.Params){
  // Display New Image Form
}
```

Because of the way we wrote our middleware, requests will be served in the order they were added. If a request matches an unauthenticated route, it will be handled. If it doesn't it will pass to the next handler in the chain, which is the `Authenticate-Request` handler. If the request is not authenticated, it will be redirected to the login page and no more handlers will be called; otherwise if the user is logged in, it will then pass through to the last part of the chain, the `authenticatedRouter`, which will then attempt to match the request.

You may have noticed that in our `NewRouter` function we're assigning an empty handler function to the router's `NotFound` property. If we don't do this, the router will render a `404 Not Found` response if no route matches a request. Since this would write to the request, our middleware would stop processing. By adding a custom `NotFound` handler that doesn't write to the response, our middleware will continue on to the next handler in the chain.

Summary

So after all of that, we've managed to cover off the fundamental basics that any decent web application requires. We know how to serve up static files, so JavaScript, CSS, and images are taken care of. We've created a Middleware so that we can add as many different handlers as we'd like to be processed, and which can be built up to handle complex situations. We've discovered how our templates are going to be handled, including adding a simple yet powerful layout functionality that reduces the amount of boilerplate code we need to write. Lastly, we've included a full-featured router that simplifies how we handle requests and how we retrieve information from the requested URL.

In the next chapter, we'll actually explore the details of what makes our web application tick: signing up users, storing users' accounts, and keeping users logged in across requests.

Gophr Part 2: All About the Users

In this chapter we're going to continue developing our new web app, Gophr. In the last chapter we set up the skeleton of our project, the folder structure, templates, assets, and middleware. Now we can attack the interesting stuff: how to handle users. As part of this we'll cover what our users look like, including generating unique IDs. We'll look at how to store user passwords and how to create a `UserStore` interface to both save and search for users.

This may sound like a small amount to be covering, but it isn't as simple as it sounds. There are a few complexities to setting up a good system, such as how we store and authenticate passwords, so to start off we'll stick to creating a simplified user system.

Before We Start

In this chapter we're going to flesh out our application. In the previous example we had a look at how our `main` function might look, but it was more of an example than real code that we can continue to use. We need to lock this in place before going any further. If you're yet to start coding along with the examples, there's a starting point codebase available in the code directory for this chapter.

So, what do we need to get up and running? For the moment, just a router for our handlers and a static file server. As we progress we'll add in authentication and a secured router, but it's unnecessary for the minute so we'll keep it simple:

1_router/main.go *(excerpt)*

```go
func main(){
    router := NewRouter()

    router.Handle("GET", "/", HandleHome)

    router.ServeFiles(
        "/assets/*filepath",
        http.Dir("assets/"),
    )

    middleware := Middleware{}
    middleware.Add(router)
    log.Fatal(http.ListenAndServe(":3000", middleware))
}
```

Okay, we're set to go.

What do users look like?

A user account in one system is often different from a user account in another system. Sometimes you're required to enter your full name and address, sometimes just a username, and sometimes nothing at all. Most of the time, I find web applications ask me for too much information, which is annoying. We'll be keeping it to the bare minimum with Gophr, and just ask for a username, email address, and password. This way we're able to identify users by a unique username, contact them via email, and authenticate them with a password.

If we were to create a user type for what I've just described, it might look a little like this:

```
type User struct {
    Username string
    Email    string
    Password string
}
```

Some of you may have already picked up that storing a password in a user entity is a bad idea, and you'd be right. We should *never* store a user's password—and I mean *never*. There's no reason for us to store the password without modification. If we're storing it, we're responsible for its security, and it opens us up to unnecessary risk. A password doesn't have to be in its raw form, so we'll store a hash of the password instead.

A hashing algorithm is a one-way transformation that turns a password into another string. Once we have the hashed value of a string, such as a password, we're unable to get the original string back. It's safe to store the hash of a password; when a user attempts to log in, we can hash the password they provide and check if it matches the hash we have stored for them. This means we can say whether a supplied string is the same as the user's password without actually storing the password itself. We'll look more at hashing algorithms shortly.

So our user type looks slightly different now that we're storing the hashed password rather than the password itself:

```
type User struct{
    Username       string
    Email          string
    HashedPassword string
}
```

Hashing a Password

 ## Hashing Algorithm Tips

Over the last decade or so, it's become a well-known problem in the web industry that many websites use a hashing algorithm that is unsecured, or do not "salt" their hashes. Hashing algorithms such as MD5 or SHA1 once were commonplace, but are now considered insecure. By the same token a lot of sites stored just the hash of the password, which meant that hackers could create a database of hashes of common words or passwords (called a "rainbow table"), then easily look up the password if they were able to access a hash . Nowadays hashes are expected to be **salted**, which means adding random characters to the password before hashing it, then storing those characters alongside the hashed password. This way it's very unlikely that somebody will already have a precomputed hash of the password and the salt, and will have to try cracking each password individually.

We'll be using the hashing algorithm BCrypt. This is a secure and well-accepted hashing algorithm. There are a few viable alternatives, and you're welcome to do research and use a different algorithm if you're so inclined. BCrypt is a good algorithm because, unlike many well-used algorithms, it's designed specifically for the task and has a configurable "cost" that determines how long the hashing takes. By making sure your hashing is quite slow, say 30-50ms, you're able to prevent attackers from trying hundreds of thousands of password combinations quickly, and that keeps your users' passwords safe.

Identifiers

We're going to require a unique internal identifier, a user ID of sorts. Generating unique IDs is an important part of any web application. We'll have to generate them for a variety of objects, so it's important we use the right type of ID!

While, historically, a lot of applications have defaulted to using an incrementing primary key—where each ID receives the next number in line—these days fewer predictable IDs are in use.

A common, non-incremental ID type is the UUID or **universally unique identifier**. There are a few versions of the UUID, but version 4 is commonly used in web applications. Version 4 UUIDs are randomly generated and use the format "xxxxxxxx-xxxx-4xxx-yxxx-xxxxxxxxxxxx," where x is any hexadecimal character and y is one of 8, 9, A, or B; for example: 362126c8-7fdd-4e4c-9c5a-faeb0ef14d63.

While you can choose to use UUIDs, I find them a little … uh … verbose for my liking. I prefer something more concise (albeit with less entropy). For Gophr, we're going to use a prefixed, random alphanumeric identifier of varying length. For instance, a user ID will have the prefix usr, and have 16 characters, such as "usr_CCzeF4JB0VzfC1Jv." By making the length variable, we're able to use smaller IDs when fewer records are likely to be created (such as for users), and longer IDs when more records will be created (such as for our images). This means we avoid adding unnecessary entropy, and making our URLs unnecessarily long and ugly.

 Entropy

> **Entropy** is the level of randomness; the more random characters in our ID, the more entropy it has. It's important to have enough entropy to avoid encountering many collisions or duplicate IDs. For example, with 62 alphanumeric characters available, an ID with only eight characters will have 62^8 possible permutations. That's over 218 billion possible IDs. While the chance of creating the same ID twice is low, it's always best to err on the side of caution. Gophr's going to be big, too, so probably best to stick with at least ten characters of entropy.

Let's create a function that generates IDs for us. It's going to take a prefix string and a length: `func GenerateID(prefix string, length int) string`. Inside we'll create an array of bytes with a capacity equal to the length we require, then use the `rand.Read` function to fill the byte array with random numbers. Once we have an array of random numbers, we can loop through it and replace each random number with an alphanumeric character. Finally, we can return the formatted string with its prefix:

2_registration/id.go

```go
package main

import (
    "crypto/rand"
    "fmt"
)

// Source String used when generating a random identifier.
const idSource = "0123456789ABCDEFGHIJKLMNOPQRSTUVWXYZabcdefghijklmn
➥opqrstuvwxyz"

// Save the length in a constant so we don't look it up each time.
const idSourceLen = byte(len(idSource))

// GenerateID creates a prefixed random identifier.
func GenerateID(prefix string, length int) string {
    // Create an array with the correct capacity
    id := make([]byte, length)
    // Fill our array with random numbers
```

```
rand.Read(id)

// Replace each random number with an alphanumeric value
for i, b := range id {
    id[i] = idSource[b%idSourceLen]
}

// Return the formatted id
return fmt.Sprintf("%s_%s", prefix, string(id))
}
```

The trickiest bit here is the line `id[i] = idSource[b%idSourceLen]`, which is replacing the random number in the array with a random alphanumeric character. `b%idSourceLen` ensures that the random number is no higher than the length of our alphanumeric character string `idSource` by using the remainder of the random number divided by the number of characters from which we have to choose. By accessing the string as if it were an array `idSource[indexNumber]`, we're just assigning the character at that index offset. For example, `idSource[12]` would be the character `B`.

 Pseudo-random Number Generators

> The Go standard library provides a cryptographically sound **pseudo-random number generator**, or PSRNG. Not all languages do this, and you should always double-check how sound a random number generator is. For identifiers, this is not such a problem, but if you were generating random values used to secure information, it might make a difference.

User Forms

Okay, cool, now we can hash a password and generate an ID. That will only go so far in the real world, but they're important fundamentals to have under our belt. Next up we're going to actually look at something we can *see*—the registration, account editing, and sign-in forms.

Account registration will ask for the username, email, and password. The account editing page will have the same fields, but also an **old password** field to ensure that only users who know their password can change their password (just in case you forget to log out and another person tries to change it. Oh, did I say "you"? I meant "they"). The sign-in page will just ask for a username and password.

Creating Users

When we visit /register, we'll serve up a registration form. This will also be the path to which we submit the form, but since it will be a POST HTTP request rather than a GET request, we'll be processing the request with a different handler.

Registration Form

Any form responsible for creating or updating an entity, such as a user, has similar functionality. We have to be able to enter or modify data, check the entered data's validity, and display error messages back to the user if the data is incorrect.

For our registration form, we'll let users enter their username, email, and password—and have a space to display an error message.

Let's put our template in **templates/users/new.html** and, following our naming convention, call it users/new:

```
{{define "users/new"}}
<div class="col-md-6 col-md-offset-3">
    <h1>Sign Up</h1>
    <form action="/register" method="POST">
        ...
        <input type="submit" value="Register" class="btn
➥btn-primary">
    </form>
</div>
{{end}}
```

We're wrapping our form in a div element with two classes. col-md-6 makes this div span six columns. Since the Bootstrap grid system has a width of 12 columns, this means it has a width of 50% of the page. By adding col-md-offset-3 we're saying to offset the div by three columns, effectively positioning the div in the centre of the page.

Next up, we'll add the actual input elements. To format these nicely with Bootstrap, we wrap each label and input with a div element with class form-group, and add a class of form-control to each input element:

```
<div class="form-group">
    <label for="newUsername">Username</label>
    <input type="text" name="username" id="newUsername" class=
➥"form-control">
</div>
```

Our last task is to make sure that if some user data is passed to the form, we display it as the input value. This would happen if a validation error occurred, since we don't want the user to have to re–enter a username if their email address is invalid. The only input we won't do this for is the password:

```
<div class="form-group">
    <label for="newUsername">Username</label>
    <input type="text" name="username" value="{{.User.Username}}"
➥id="newUsername" class="form-control">
</div>
```

If we add this all together, with all of our inputs, we produce a form that looks like this in **templates/users/new.html**:

```
{{define "users/new"}}
<div class="col-md-6 col-md-offset-3">
    <h1>Sign Up</h1>
    <form action="/register" method="POST">
        <div class="form-group">
            <label for="newUsername">Username</label>
            <input type="text" name="username" value="{{.User.
➥Username}}" id="newUsername" class="form-control">
        </div>
        <div class="form-group">
            <label for="newEmail">Email</label>
            <input type="text" name="email" value="{{.User.Email}}"
➥id="newEmail" class="form-control">
        </div>
        <div class="form-group">
            <label for="newPassword">Password</label>
            <input type="password" name="password" id="newPassword"
➥class="form-control">
        </div>
        <input type="submit" value="Register" class="btn
➥btn-primary">
```

```
        </form>
    </div>
{{end}}
```

The only task left to do is to display an error if there is one:

```
{{define "users/new"}}
<div class="col-md-6 col-md-offset-3">
    <h1>Sign Up</h1>
    {{if .Error}}
    <p class="text-danger">
        {{.Error}}
    </p>
    {{end}}
    <form action="/register" method="POST">
        <div class="form-group">
            <label for="newUsername">Username</label>
            <input type="text" name="username" value="{{.User.
➥Username}}" id="newUsername" class="form-control">
        </div>
        <div class="form-group">
            <label for="newEmail">Email</label>
            <input type="text" name="email" value="{{.User.Email}}"
➥id="newEmail" class="form-control">
        </div>
        <div class="form-group">
            <label for="newPassword">Password</label>
            <input type="password" name="password" id="newPassword"
➥class="form-control">
        </div>
        <input type="submit" value="Register" class="btn
➥btn-primary">
    </form>
</div>
{{end}}
```

Registration Handler

Now that we have a form, we need a handler to serve it up. Our user handlers will sit in the **handle_user.go** file. We'll try and keep our handler functions in files that start with handle so that we can easily find them. Our HandleUserNew function is straightforward:

```
                                    2_registration/handle_user.go (excerpt)
func HandleUserNew(w http.ResponseWriter, r *http.Request, _
➥httprouter.Params) {
    RenderTemplate(w, r, "users/new", nil)
}
```

You can see that we're using a `httprouter` handle function, as it has the third
parameter of type `httprouter.Params`. As we won't be using it, we can ignore it by
assigning it to the blank identifier `_`. Lastly, we'll add this to our router, in **main.go**:

```
router.Handle("GET", "/register", HandleUserNew)
```

If you compile your code and view `http://127.0.0.1:3000/register` in a browser,
you'll see a beautiful registration form as can be seen in Figure 5.1.

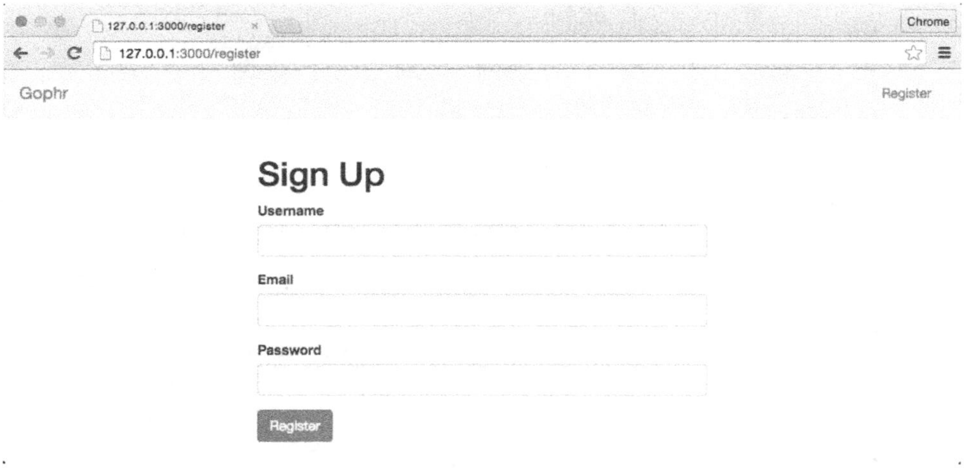

Figure 5.1. Our beautiful registration form

You will, however, notice that if you submit the form, you'll receive a **404** error.
That's because we're yet to write a handler for the post, so it's time we do that now.

Creating Users

To create a user, we combine everything we've learned in this chapter about users,
password hashes, and IDs into a single function. Then we add a nice way to handle
errors when things go wrong.

It's quite easy to bundle this all up into a single function: NewUser(username, email, password string) (User, error). We'll pass in the user attributes and get a User or error back.

Input Validation

Input validation is probably the trickiest area, and most open to interpretation. For Gophr, we'll keep it simple and have a special error type ValidationError. This type will be based on the error type, and can be returned from NewUser. We can check the error type in the handler and perform different actions if the error is a validation error.

We can create specific errors up front that are returned when a validation issue is encountered. This is a good way to have named errors placed in a single area of the code. Let's create validation errors for common user sign-up issues:

```
                                              2_registration/errors.go (excerpt)

type ValidationError error

var (
    errNoUsername         = ValidationError(errors.New("You must
➥supply a username"))
    errNoEmail            = ValidationError(errors.New("You must
➥supply an email"))
    errNoPassword         = ValidationError(errors.New("You must
➥supply a password"))
    errPasswordTooShort = ValidationError(errors.New("Your password
➥is too short"))
)

func IsValidationError(err error) bool {
    _, ok := err.(ValidationError)
    return ok
}
```

If our users encounter an error, we can return errNoUsername instead of creating a new instance of an error. We then figure out what the error message should be. This is a great way to keep all your error messages grouped together, and makes them easy to find or update.

IsValidationError Helper Function

We've also created a helper function that will return "true" if a supplied error is of the type `ValidationError`. We'll use this to differentiate between serious errors and validation errors. `IsValidationError` attempts to coerce the value to a `ValidationError`. The result is a typed value and a Boolean that lets us know if the value was able to be coerced, which we use as the return value.

Now that we know what errors might be returned, we have a good indication of what needs to be done at the start of our `NewUser` function. We'll check that all the details are provided, and that our password is of sufficient length:

2_registstration/user.go

```go
const (
    passwordLength = 8
    hashCost = 10
    userIDLength
)

func NewUser(username, email, password string) (User, error){
    user := User{
        Email:    email,
        Username: username,
    }
    if username == "" {
        return user, errNoUsername
    }

    if email == "" {
        return user, errNoEmail
    }

    if password == "" {
        return user, errNoPassword
    }

    if len(password) < passwordLength {
        return user, errPasswordTooShort
    }
    hashedPassword, err := bcrypt.GenerateFromPassword([]byte
➥(password), hashCost)
```

```
    user.HashedPassword = string(hashedPassword)
    user.ID = GenerateID("usr", userIDLength)

    return user, err
}
```

This should all be self-explanatory, except that you might be wondering why we return the user—even if there is a validation error! This allows us to provide a user object to the registration form users/new. In our HTML inputs we display back to the browser the username or email that has been entered . Without returning the user, we'd have no easy way to pass that information to the template.

So how do we use this function? Well, we need to add in a handler for a POST request to /register. In the handler we'll attempt to create a new user, check if there is a validation error, and redisplay the form if there is:

2_registration/main.go (excerpt)

```
// Add the route handler
router.Handle("POST", "/register", HandleUserCreate)
```

2_registration/handle_user.go (excerpt)

```
func HandleUserCreate(w http.ResponseWriter, r *http.Request, _
➡httprouter.Params) {
    // Process creating a user
}
```

We can retrieve a form value by name using the method FormValue(key string) on the request. We use this method to get the username, email, and password, which we pass as the parameters to NewUser:

2_registration/handle_user.go *(excerpt)*

```go
user, err := NewUser(
    r.FormValue("username"),
    r.FormValue("email"),
    r.FormValue("password"),
)
```

Now that we've passed our values to the `NewUser` function, we check to see if a validation error occurred. Not only must we know if it's an error, but we also need to know if it's a validation error:

2_registration/handle_user.go *(excerpt)*

```go
if err != nil {
    if IsValidationError(err) {
        RenderTemplate(w, r, "users/new", map[string]
➥interface{}{
            "Error": err.Error(),
            "User":  user,
        })
        return
    }
    panic(err)
}

http.Redirect(w, r, "/?flash=User+created", http.StatusFound)
```

By checking if the `error` is a `ValidationError`, we're able to re-render the `users/new` template, but this time we provide a user and error value to be rendered. Since `RenderTemplate` accepts any old data, we create a `map[string]interface{}`, which lets us store any data we want as a key, then add the `User` and `Error` values the template expects.

If you compile and run this code now, you'll be able to submit the registration form and see any validation errors appear above it. If you submit a valid user, it will simply redirect you to the home page with a query string message `User created`. We're yet to do anything with that value, but it's a good guide as to which part of your code has run.

Persisting Users

Next up, we'll look at actually doing something with the user we've created. There are two parts to this: saving the user to some sort of persistent store, and logging the user in so that we know who they are the next time they request a page. We'll look at part one of that now, persisting users when they sign up by creating a UserStore type that saves and retrieves persisted users.

For the moment, we'll just save the users into a file as JSON. This is a quick and easy way for us to save and load data, and also helps us become familiar with marshalling and unmarshalling JSON.

In later chapters, we'll look at storing data into a database using Go's database/sql package. Because we know we'll be changing the persistent store layer from file to database, we're going to implement our UserStore object as an interface rather than as a single concrete implementation. This way we can have a FileUserStore type now that implements the UserStore interface, then later on create a MySQLUserStore or PostgresUserStore depending on the database we use (spoiler alert: it's MySQL).

 ### The UserStore Interface

By making the UserStore type an interface, we'll be able to swap the concrete implementation from a file-based class to a database class and none of the other code cares. We could even do it at runtime; for example, loading in a configuration file that says which type of database class to use. This flexibility is especially powerful if you were thinking about writing your application for other users to deploy.

Our UserStore interface requires only a few methods: one to save users, and a few finder methods for retrieving users:

```
                                        3_user_store/user_store.go (excerpt)

type UserStore interface {
    Find(string) (*User, error)
    FindByEmail(string) (*User, error)
```

```
    FindByUsername(string) (*User, error)
    Save(User) error
}
```

The three finder methods will be employed to look up a user based on the unique fields each user has. `Find` will find a user based on their unique ID, whereas `FindByEmail` and `FindByUsername` allow us to look up a user by other data. We'll use these latter two methods to add more validation when creating a user, to avoid having any two users with the same username or email address.

The `Save` method is uncomplicated: it is responsible for saving a user to the `UserStore`. Easy.

Next, we create a type that implements the `UserStore` interface by saving users as JSON to a file. To do this we require two bits of information: the name of the file to save to, and a map of users that we'll use in the finder methods. The map key will be the user's ID:

3_user_store/user_store.go (excerpt)

```go
type FileUserStore struct {
    filename string
    Users    map[string]User
}
```

As you can see, the filename is not an exported field since it starts with a lowercase letter. By doing this, we won't have to worry about it showing up in the file when we marshal the store to JSON.

So now we'll start adding the methods that will make `FileUserStore` satisfy the `UserStore` interface. Let's look at `Save` first. When we save a user, we want to add it to the array of users, as well as marshall the users to the file, so if the process were to stop no information will be missing.

 Dealing with Files

Like most languages, Go provides some utility methods to make simple operations with files a little easier. We're going to use those methods, rather than deal with the complexity and verbosity that can occur with lower-level access functions. This makes sense in context of our Gophr project, but you should always evaluate what's appropriate depending on the project's requirements. Some examples of different requirements are around locking files, appending rather than overwriting files, and keeping files open for extended periods of time.

We've already seen in previous chapters how to marshal a type into JSON, so the only new code here is writing the content to a file. The io/ioutil package contains some helper methods for dealing with files, and we'll use the function ioutil.WriteFile(name string, contents []byte, permissions os.FileMode) to write the file. This function simplifies the process of writing to a file; we simply supply the name of the file, its contents as an array of bytes, and the permissions the file should have:

3_user_store/user_store.go (excerpt)

```
func (store FileUserStore) Save(user User) error {
    store.Users[user.ID] = user

    contents, err := json.MarshalIndent(store, "", "   ")
    if err != nil {
        return err
    }

    err = ioutil.WriteFile(store.filename, contents, 0660)
    if err != nil {
        return err
    }
    return nil
}
```

os.FileMode Permissions

Permissions can be written as the standard Unix octal digits you'd use with the chmod command. If you're unfamiliar with chmod, that's okay. For the moment we'll just be using permissions 0660, which will allow a user—and anyone in the same group as the user—to read and write to the file. A different user outside this group will be unable to do anything with the file.

At this point we can save a user to the store, and that saves the users to the file. Next we add the finder methods. The Find method is the simplest, as we can return the value from the map directly using the supplied ID as the lookup (the user ID is the key for the map). For the other finders, we'll just loop through all the users looking for a match:

```
3_user_store/user_store.go (excerpt)
func (store FileUserStore) Find(id string) (*User, error) {
    user, ok := store.Users[id]
    if ok {
        return &user, nil
    }
    return nil, nil
}

func (store FileUserStore) FindByUsername(username string) (*User,
➥error) {
    if username == "" {
        return nil, nil
    }

    for _, user := range store.Users {
        if strings.ToLower(username) == strings.ToLower(user.
➥Username) {
            return &user, nil
        }
    }
    return nil, nil
}

func (store FileUserStore) FindByEmail(email string) (*User,
➥error) {
    if email == "" {
        return nil, nil
    }

    for _, user := range store.Users {
        if strings.ToLower(email) == strings.ToLower(user.Email) {
            return &user, nil
        }
    }
    return nil, nil
}
```

As you can see, each function is similar. First, we're checking that the input isn't an empty string, which means we can return quickly if it's a request that's never going to find a user. After that we loop through each of the users in the store, and check if the email matches. We run the `string.ToLower` function against both the input value the value on the user object to ensure that the match is case-insensitive. We want to avoid having two users with the same username or email address but with different capitalization. If a user matches, we immediately return that user, otherwise code execution will flow through all the way to the end, where we return a `nil` value.

Returned Errors

You might be wondering why our finder methods return an error, but we're always returning `nil`. This may not make sense right now but a different implementation of `UserStore`, such as one that connects to a database, may return errors on these methods. Because we have to cater for both our `FileUserStore` and any future implementation of `UserStore`, we're making sure that the method signatures are appropriate and future-proof.

To create an actual instance of `FileUserStore` we'll need to create a `NewFileUser-Store` function to call. We'll use this function to load and return a `FileUserStore` from a specific file. To do this we'll read the file in, and unmarshall it into the `FileUserStore`'s `Users` map:

3_user_store/user_store.go (excerpt)

```go
func NewFileUserStore(filename string) (*FileUserStore, error) {
    store := &FileUserStore{
        Users:    map[string]User{},
        filename: filename,
    }

    contents, err := ioutil.ReadFile(filename)

    if err != nil {
        // If it's a matter of the file not existing, that's ok
        if os.IsNotExist(err) {
            return store, nil
        }
        return nil, err
    }
    err = json.Unmarshal(contents, store)
    if err != nil {
```

```
        return nil, err
    }
    return store, nil
}
```

The first part of this function creates a new `FileUserStore` object for us to return. After that it uses another `io.ioutil` function `ReadFile(filename string) ([]byte, error)` to read the contents of the file. This method will return an error if it can't read the file. If this is simply because the file is yet to exist, we can ignore the error, so we use `os.IsNotExists(err error) bool` to check to see if the error indicates the file doesn't exist. This function checks that the error isn't one of a variety of errors that represent a file not being able to be read, and saves us having to know or care about these different types of errors. If the file fails to exist, we just return the empty store object. If we do have the contents of the file, we try to unmarshal that into the store object, which will restore our persisted users.

So we've ticked off all the methods of the `FileUserStore` object, and we know how to create an instance of the store. next, we need to figure out how we're going to create and access an instance of `FileUserStore` within our application. Since Gophr is starting small, we're going to use a globally accessible variable, initialized at the top of `user_store.go`. We'll create an empty variable of type `UserStore` called `globalUserStore`, then in an `init` function, create a new `FileUserStore` object and place it in `globalUserStore`. You can create a function called `init` in any Go file, and it will be run as part of the initialization phase of your application—it's unnecessary to call it explicitly.

 Global Contexts

It's often considered bad practice to have a bunch of global variables floating around, but for the purpose of this project, it's perfectly acceptable. Having a large number of global values can quickly become hard to maintain, and conflicts may arise. If Gophr were to become much more complex, you might look at alternatives for managing a `UserStore` dependency, but for the moment we're going with a simple solution.

We're going to store our users in the file `data/users.json`, so please take the time now to create the directory `data`, otherwise you'll come up across some errors later on!

```
                                      3_user_store/user_store.go (excerpt)

var globalUserStore UserStore

func init() {
    store, err := NewFileUserStore("./data/users.json")
    if err != nil {
        panic(fmt.Errorf("Error creating user store: %s", err))
    }
    globalUserStore = store
}
```

First, we're creating a new variable `store` of type `FileUserStore`; then we're placing it in `globalUserStore`, which is a variable of interface `UserStore`. This is okay because `FileUserStore` implements `UserStore` by defining the correct methods. At this point, you should be able to compile the code and run it; however, we've yet to hook up the `HandleUserCreate` function to use the `globalUserStore`, so no functionality has actually changed.

We can also hook up our `HandleUserCreate` to use the `globalUserStore`. Not only do we save the user we create, we also check to see that there are no users with the same username or email address before creating our user. To do this we add a couple of extra validation errors:

```
                                          3_user_store/errors.go (excerpt)

var (
    errNoUsername       = ValidationError(errors.New("You must
➥supply a username"))
    errNoEmail          = ValidationError(errors.New("You must
➥supply an email"))
    errNoPassword       = ValidationError(errors.New("You must
➥supply a password"))
    errPasswordTooShort = ValidationError(errors.New("Your password
➥is too short"))
    errUsernameExists   = ValidationError(errors.New("That username
➥is taken"))
    errEmailExists      = ValidationError(errors.New("That email
➥address has an account"))
)
```

Now we validate that no user exists with either the same username or email. This code goes in the function `NewUser` after we check the length of the password:

```
                                    3_user_store/user.go (excerpt)

    // Check if the username exists
    existingUser, err := globalUserStore.FindByUsername(username)
    if err != nil {
        return user, err
    }
    if existingUser != nil {
        return user, errUsernameExists
    }

    // Check if the email exists
    existingUser, err = globalUserStore.FindByEmail(email)
    if err != nil {
        return user, err
    }
    if existingUser != nil {
        return user, errEmailExists
    }
```

Just as how the `FindByEmail` and `FindByUsername` functions are alike, their validation is similar too. We ask for the user by email and username and then check for errors; if we've returned an existing user we throw an appropriate validation error. Our final task is to update our `HandleCreateUser` handler to persist the user, and we're good to go! At the end of the function, just before the `http.Redirect`, save the user:

```
                              3_user_store/handle_user.go (excerpt)

    err = globalUserStore.Save(user)
    if err != nil {
        panic(err)
    }
```

You can compile your code now, and when you add a user you should see **data/users.json** be updated with that user information. Be careful when opening that file to check, though, as you may need to close it again before Gophr can write to it. Here's what mine looked like after adding a few users:

```
{
  "Users": {
    "usr_YF7PZoy7f2p9ZbKZ": {
      "ID": "usr_YF7PZoy7f2p9ZbKZ",
```

```
        "Email": "mal@mal.co.nz",
        "HashedPassword": "$2a$10$kqGFMOEsp.RwD3OC75AzmOOJCpXH9IYrzCx
↪GAaF6vqHsJ7PngctEy",
        "Username": "mal"
    },
    "usr_nf9RUQN328ILODbh": {
        "ID": "usr_nf9RUQN328ILODbh",
        "Email": "malevolent@mal.co.nz",
        "HashedPassword": "$2a$10$sYroqL1aXtMDGh.MX/lUVe1/Nvk5Zig4oWC8
↪GKTzJ2cr8zCXIkMKy",
        "Username": "malevolent"
    },
    "usr_nfY9lTrAlBQNXtNv": {
        "ID": "usr_nfY9lTrAlBQNXtNv",
        "Email": "malnourished@mal.co.nz",
        "HashedPassword": "$2a$10$LtNPyUq4TbKa2JE7SjVOa.OSFMybbAvkHdnM
↪2jpa3db5SkLDBEi3S",
        "Username": "malnourished"
    }
  }
}
```

Summary

In this chapter we covered the basics of our user system. We're now able to sign up for Gophr and create a new user. Not only are we creating users, but we're validating the input to ensure that we have correct values and avoid creating duplicate users. We're also storing and loading our users from a file, so we can persist users across restarts of the app.

In the next chapter we'll look at how we keep those users logged in, and how we can let users come back and sign in to their account.

Exercises

If you're feeling like it's all a bit easy in this chapter, I have a few extra credit exercises for you:

- Increase the performance of `FindByEmail` and `FindByUsername` by creating separate maps that use the email or username as the key, so that you avoid looping through every user. You'll need to make sure that you add to the maps when saving a user, and somehow input data into them when you load the file from the file system.

Refactor the `NewUser` function so that you can return multiple validation errors. If a user fails to enter a password or email address, both of the errors should be displayed, rather than just the first one. There's a few ways to do this—I'll leave the implementation details up to you!

Gophr Part 3: Remembering Our Users

Last chapter we created our registration form, learned how to create users, and persist them to disk to avoid losing them between server restarts. We still have to cover how to keep them logged into Gophr. Since HTTP is a **stateless protocol**—in that it fails to remember anything about you from one request to the next—we use another means to track users between requests: cookies.

In this chapter, we'll create a session system that lets users log in and out of Gophr at their discretion. To do this, we assign users a session that we store on the server side. Each session has a unique identifier, which is returned to the user in a cookie so that we can match the cookie in the request to the session. The cookie will have an expiry time, as will the session information that we store on the server (the same time). Adding an expiry time to a session and extending it when a user visits a page lets us add a little security to our system. Without an expiry time, a session ID becomes a token enabling neverending access to a user's account—definitely not what you want to be leaving on a user's computer forever.

Once we have the ability to track a user via a session, we'll add a handler to our middleware that checks to see if a user is logged in; then we'll add another router to the middleware that will have all of our authenticated routes. This enables us to have public routes, which anybody can access, and private routes, which are only available if a user is logged in.

What makes up a session?

A **session** can be used to store any information we choose. Since we'll be defining a session type, we can add any fields we want. For Gophr, the only information we'll require at this point is the user that we want to keep logged in. So, along with the identifier and expiry values, our session type looks like this:

1_new_session/session.go (excerpt)

```go
type Session struct {
    ID     string
    UserID string
    Expiry time.Time
}
```

We need to know how long to keep a session active for, and the name of the cookie that we store it in, so let's define a couple of constants with those values:

1_new_session/session.go (excerpt)

```go
const (
    // Keep users logged in for 3 days
    sessionLength     = 24 * 3 * time.Hour
    sessionCookieName = "GophrSession"
    sessionIDLength   = 20
)
```

 A Lack of Days

The Go time package has predefined constants for time up to an hour, but not for days or longer periods. There are several reasons for this, such as days being able to transition across daylight savings, to aspects such as leap seconds. The underlying reason is the same: the length of a day changes, so there is no constant value that represents a day. Go does provide plenty of tools to deal with dates that have more context than a simple duration. Just multiplying 24 hours by three will give us a duration close enough to three days for our purposes.

Next up, we'll create a session. We'll define a function for this, which not only creates a session object but also takes an `http.ResponseWriter` to write a cookie to. Cookies are easily managed with the type `http.Cookie` and function `http.Set-Cookie(http.ResponseWriter, *http.Cookie)`. The cookie, and the session itself, will share an expiry date. We can reuse our `GenerateID` function to create our session IDs:

```
                                                 1_new_session/session.go (excerpt)
func NewSession(w http.ResponseWriter) *Session {
    expiry := time.Now().Add(sessionLength)

    session := &Session{
        ID:     GenerateID("sess", sessionIDLength),
        Expiry: expiry,
    }

    cookie := http.Cookie{
        Name:    sessionCookieName,
        Value:   session.ID,
        Expires: expiry,
    }

    http.SetCookie(w, &cookie)
    return session
}
```

So we've defined the expiry variable as a time by adding the duration `sessionLength` to the current time, returned from `time.Now()`. Next up we create a new `http.Cookie` instance. `http.Cookie` has a variety of fields that I won't cover here; instead we'll just focus on the parts we're using for the moment. If you're interested in more, check out the HTTP package website.[1] The cookie has a name, value, and expiry. The name will be `GophrSession` and the value will be the session ID. Adding the expiry will enable your browser to delete the cookie after the supplied date.

Finally, we write the cookie to the `http.ResponseWriter` passed to the function as a parameter with the function `http.SetCookie`. It's unnecessary to know about the internals of this function, just that it ensures the cookie information will be returned as a header in the response.

---

[1] http://golang.org/pkg/net/http/#Cookie

From here we can adapt our `HandleUserCreate` function to create a new session when we sign up a user, and then add the user to that session. Currently, we lack the ability to store sessions between requests, but at least we'll be able to see our session cookie getting set!

Find your `HandleUserCreate` function and call the `NewSession` method after saving our new user but before redirecting the response. Now add the user to the session that's returned:

1_new_session/handle_user.go (excerpt)

```
err = globalUserStore.Save(&user)
if err != nil {
    RenderError(w, err)
    return
}

// Create a new session
session := NewSession(w)
session.UserID = user.ID

http.Redirect(w, r, "/?flash=User+created", http.StatusFound)
```

Compile your code, and when you create a user, the return response will have a `Set-Cookie` header. You can check this out via the command line with cURL if you'd like:

```
curl -X POST --data "username=mal&email=mal@mal.co.nz&password=
➡password" -D - http://127.0.0.1:3000/register
```

```
HTTP/1.1 302 Found
Location: /?flash=User+created
Set-Cookie: GophrSession=sess_nD1BJQbpG5KZlYoj2477; Expires=Thu,
➡04 Jun 2015 08:31:16 UTC
```

```
Date: Mon, 01 Jun 2015 08:31:16 GMT
Content-Length: 0
Content-Type: text/plain; charset=utf-8
```

Persisting User Sessions

Sessions are of little use if they fail to retain their data between requests—I mean, that's all they're good for! To make this work, we save our sessions to disk and have a SessionStore type that's responsible for storing and retrieving sessions. We've already done this once with the UserStore—we wrote code that writes marshalled JSON to a file and reads it back in when we start the app—so the code will look very familiar. First we'll create a SessionStore interface with some lookup methods; then we'll create a concrete implementation that saves and reads from a file in the data directory:

2_session_store/session_store.go (excerpt)

```
type SessionStore interface {
    Find(string) (*Session, error)
    Save(*Session) error
    Delete(*Session) error
}
```

Our SessionStore interface defines methods to find, save, and delete sessions:

2_session_store/session_store.go (excerpt)

```
type FileSessionStore struct {
    filename string
    Sessions map[string]Session
}

func NewFileSessionStore(name string) (*FileSessionStore, error) {
    store := &FileSessionStore{
        Sessions: map[string]Session{},
        filename: name,
    }

    contents, err := ioutil.ReadFile(name)

    if err != nil {
        // If it's a matter of the file not existing, that's ok
```

```
        if os.IsNotExist(err) {
            return store, nil
        }
        return nil, err
    }
    err = json.Unmarshal(contents, store)
    if err != nil {
        return nil, err
    }
    return store, err
}
```

Now we've defined a concrete implementation type, `FileSessionStore`, and implemented a function to create a new store at the supplied file path. Lastly, we'll implement the remaining `SessionStore` interface methods:

2_session_store/session_store.go (excerpt)

```
func (s *FileSessionStore) Find(id string) (*Session, error) {
    session, exists := s.Sessions[id]
    if !exists {
        return nil, nil
    }

    return &session, nil
}

func (store *FileSessionStore) Save(session *Session) error {
    contents, err := json.MarshalIndent(store, "", "  ")
    if err != nil {
        return err
    }

    return ioutil.WriteFile(store.filename, contents, 0660)
}

func (store *FileSessionStore) Delete(session *Session) error {
    delete(store.Sessions, session.ID)
    contents, err := json.MarshalIndent(store, "", "  ")
    if err != nil {
        return err
    }
```

```
    return ioutil.WriteFile(store.filename, contents, 0660)
}
```

The Find and Save methods are fairly identical to our FileUserStore methods of the same name in the previous chapter, but the Delete method is a new one. All this method does is delete the session from the Sessions map in the store and then save the store to file. Once a session is deleted from the store, it will no longer be found on future requests, so we'll need to ensure we delete the cookie after we use it.

The only task left to do is to create an instance of FileUserStore and save our session to it. Once we've done that, we're able to retrieve the session on future page requests and figure out which user is requesting the page:

2_session_store/session_store.go (excerpt)

```
var globalSessionStore SessionStore

func init() {
    sessionStore, err := NewFileSessionStore("./data/sessions.json")
    if err != nil {
        panic(fmt.Errorf("Error creating session store: %s", err))
    }
    globalSessionStore = sessionStore
}
```

2_session_store/handle_user.go (excerpt)

```
// Create a new session
session := NewSession(w)
session.UserID = user.ID
err = globalSessionStore.Save(session)
if err != nil {
    panic(err)
}
```

At this point you should be able to compile and run your code, visit the sign-up page, create a user, and then see the data file be created in **data/sessions.json**. If you view this file, it'll look a little like this:

```
{
  "Sessions": {
    "sess_GBEX1QxONXmSgXL1nPDg": {
      "ID": "sess_GBEX1QxONXmSgXL1nPDg",
      "UserID": "usr_CydtIC9KUZGOCbjx",
      "Expiry": "2015-06-04T21:52:36.144147885+13:00"
    }
  }
}
```

Next up, we'll create a middleware handler that checks if a user is logged in, and then lets them edit their account if they are.

Checking for a User

To check if a request has a signed-in user attached to it, we read the session cookie from the request and load the session if possible. Once we've loaded the session from the `SessionStore`, we can see if there's a user ID attached to the session and retrieve that user from the `UserStore`. If all goes well, we can let the request continue on.

Let's start by creating two new functions in `session.go` that are responsible for retrieving either a `Session` or `User` from the request:

3_require_login/session.go (excerpt)

```go
func RequestSession(r *http.Request) *Session {
    cookie, err := r.Cookie(sessionCookieName)
    if err != nil {
        return nil
    }

    session, err := globalSessionStore.Find(cookie.Value)
    if err != nil {
        panic(err)
    }

    if session == nil {
        return nil
    }

    if session.Expired() {
```

```
          globalSessionStore.Delete(session)
          return nil
    }
    return session
}
```

You'll see that we're asking for the `GophrSession` cookie from the request. If it exists, we retrieve the session from the `globalSessionStore` and return it. We've also added a call to see whether the session has expired—except we're yet to write that function. Let's do that now:

```
                                              3_require_login/session.go (excerpt)

func (session *Session) Expired() bool {
    return session.Expiry.Before(time.Now())
}
```

Okay, so now we have a function that will return a session from a request, if one exists. Let's add the `RequestUser` function that takes this one step further and returns the user associated with the session:

```
                                              3_require_login/session.go (excerpt)

func RequestUser(r *http.Request) *User {
    session := RequestSession(r)
    if session == nil || session.UserID == "" {
        return nil
    }

    user, err := globalUserStore.Find(session.UserID)
    if err != nil {
        panic(err)
    }
    return user
}
```

Now we can add the final piece of the puzzle—a handler which requires a user to be logged in to continue. If there's no logged-in user, we'll redirect to a login page:

3_require_login/session.go *(excerpt)*

```go
func RequireLogin(w http.ResponseWriter, r *http.Request) {
    // Let the request pass if we've got a user
    if RequestUser(r) != nil {
        return
    }

    query := url.Values{}
    query.Add("next", url.QueryEscape(r.URL.String()))

    http.Redirect(w, r, "/login?"+query.Encode(), http.StatusFound)
}
```

Here we've defined a handler that checks whether or not `RequestUser` returns a user. If it doesn't we redirect to /`login`, and add the current request URL as the query string param `next`. By adding in the request path in the redirect, we're able to retain the URL we were trying to reach while we log in, the idea being that once we're logged in or signed up, we can continue on to the page we were trying to reach.

Displaying User Information

Before we go any further, it's time for us to kill a couple of birds with one stone. Our layout currently has a navigation bar that displays a link to the registration page. That was all well and good as a helper before, but now it needs to be a bit smarter, aware of whether or not we have a user. If a user is logged in, it should display other links such as to the sign-out page or the user's account details page.

You may also have noticed in our redirects that I've been adding messages into a query string parameter `flash`. This is a very simple implementation of flash messages, and we should be displaying these on the page when they're present. The good news is that both the current user and flash messages can be added to the template scope in one place. Once the information is passed into the template, we can easily add more logic to our templates.

 Flash Messages

Flash messages is a term used to refer to messages on the next page displayed after an action is performed. Since no page is displayed immediately and a redirect is issued, we must pass this notification somehow. Often messages are stored in a session and removed after being displayed to prevent them showing if the page is refreshed, but we'll create a simplified version using query string parameters.

To start off, let's update our `RenderTemplate` function to add in both the current user and flash message information into the data that is sent to the template:

```
                                    4_template_data/template.go (excerpt)

func RenderTemplate(w http.ResponseWriter, r *http.Request, name
➥string, data map[string]interface{}) {
    if data == nil {
        data = map[string]interface{}{}
    }

    data["CurrentUser"] = RequestUser(r)
    data["Flash"] = r.URL.Query().Get("flash")
    ...
}
```

Notice that we've changed the variable `data` from type `interface{}` to type `map[string]interface{}`. This is actually the value we've been passing through previously, but now we're being more explicit about it. By ensuring we get a map, we can add our own values to it—which is what we do next. First replace a `nil` data value with an empty map, just in case no data was passed in. After that, we add the current user in as the key `CurrentUser`. By using `CurrentUser` instead of `User`, we're being explicit about what this data actually is, ensuring there's no clash with the `User` value we assign when we're registering a user.

The `Flash` key is set to the value that comes in via the query string, which we obtain from the request URL. If this doesn't exist, it will just be an empty string, which our template will ignore.

Now we've added these values to the data that's passed into our templates, we're able to add in the required logic. We'll be adding to our layout file, since we want to write the template in one place, and one place only:

```
<html>
    <head>
        <link rel="stylesheet" href="/assets/css/bootstrap.css">
    </head>
    <body>
    <nav class="navbar navbar-default" role="navigation">
        <div class="container-fluid">
            <div class="navbar-header">
                <a class="navbar-brand" href="/">Gophr</a>
            </div>
            <div class="collapse navbar-collapse">
                <p class="navbar-text navbar-right">
                    {{if .CurrentUser}}
                    <a href="/account" class="navbar-link">Account
➡</a> |

                    <a href="/sign-out" class="navbar-link">Sign Out
➡</a>

                    {{else}}
                    <a href="/register" class="navbar-link">Register
➡</a> |

                    <a href="/login" class="navbar-link">Login</a>
                    {{end}}
                </p>
            </div>
        </div>
    </nav>
    <div class="container">
        {{if .Flash}}
            <div class="alert alert-info">
                {{.Flash}}
            </div>
        {{end}}
        {{ yield }}
        </div>
    </body>
</html>
```

As you can see, we now check whether there's a current user. If there is, we show
the **Account** and **Sign Out** links, otherwise we show **Register** and **Login**. The second
part we've added is to display the flash message inside an alert div. This will just
display inside a blue box above the rest of the content for the page.

I should note at this point that the new links we've created (**Account**, **Sign Out**, and **Login**) are yet to actually do anything—that's what we're going to build next.

If you build and run Gophr now, you're able to sign up and see that the links in the nav bar change—that's our session in action! When you visit the home page after registering, you should see the flash message **User created** as well.

HTML Escaping

This is a chance to see the Go template package's escaping in action. If you change the `flash` value in the query string to contain some HTML code (such as "`User </div> created`"), you'll notice that the flash message correctly displays the value, rather than allow the HTML in the flash message to break the page.

Signing Out, Signing In

Now that we've created an account, our users have to be able to sign out and log in when they return. Signing out is a simple enough process to do; we just delete the user's session from the session store. This essentially removes any knowledge we have about that user, who is subsequently no longer considered logged in. To log in, we do the reverse, creating a new session just like when we register a user, except that we confirm the user's details upon login, ensuring that people are who they say they are.

Currently our `main` function is as follows:

```go
func main() {
    router := NewRouter()

    router.Handle("GET", "/", HandleHome)
    router.Handle("GET", "/register", HandleUserNew)
    router.Handle("POST", "/register", HandleUserCreate)

    router.ServeFiles(
        "/assets/*filepath",
        http.Dir("assets/"),
    )

    middleware := Middleware{}
```

```
    middleware.Add(router)
    log.Fatal(http.ListenAndServe(":3000", middleware))
}
```

Since signing out should be an action that's only available to a logged-in user, it's time for us to put our `RequireLogin` handler into action. We're going to adjust our middleware stack to have a second router that's only for logged-in users. The login page can be added to the current router, however, since that's for unauthenticated users.

Here's the main function with `GET` and `POST` handlers to display a login form via `HandleSessionNew` and process the login form via `HandleSessionCreate`. We've also created a new router `secureRouter` and added a `GET` handler to sign out a user via `HandleSessionDestroy`. Lastly, we add both `RequireLogin` and our `secureRouter` to the middleware chain, ordered so that `RequireLogin` runs before any secure routes can be visited:

5_signing_out_and_in/main.go (excerpt)

```
func main() {
    router := NewRouter()

    router.Handle("GET", "/", HandleHome)
    router.Handle("GET", "/register", HandleUserNew)
    router.Handle("POST", "/register", HandleUserCreate)
    router.Handle("GET", "/login", HandleSessionNew)
    router.Handle("POST", "/login", HandleSessionCreate)

    router.ServeFiles(
        "/assets/*filepath",
        http.Dir("assets/"),
    )

    secureRouter := NewRouter()
    secureRouter("GET", "/sign-out", HandleSessionDestroy)

    middleware := Middleware{}
    middleware.Add(router)
    middleware.Add(http.HandlerFunc(RequireLogin))
    middleware.Add(secureRouter)
```

```
    log.Fatal(http.ListenAndServe(":3000", middleware))
}
```

The Sign Out Process

At this point the routes are all set up; we just need to create the handler functions, the business logic they require, and any templates that are missing. We'll start with signing out, since that's a relatively simple process.

Inside a new file called **handle_session.go**, create a new handler function `HandleSessionDestroy`. Inside this, we get the request session and check whether it exists; we delete it if it does, and then display a logged out message:

5_signing_out_and_in/handle_session.go (excerpt)

```
func HandleSessionDestroy(w http.ResponseWriter, r *http.Request, _
➥httprouter.Params) {
    session := RequestSession(r)
    if session != nil {
        err := globalSessionStore.Delete(session)
        if err != nil {
            panic(err)
        }
    }
    RenderTemplate(w, r, "sessions/destroy", nil)
}
```

And now you can add an appropriate template `sessions/destroy` in the file **templates/sessions/destroy.html**:

5_signing_out_and_in/templates/sessions/destroy.html

```
{{define "sessions/destroy"}}
<div class="row">
    <div class="col-md-6 col-md-offset-3">
        <h1>Signed Out</h1>
        <p>Thanks, you're now signed out.</p>
        <p><a href="/login">Login</a></p>
```

```
    </div>
  </div>
{{end}}
```

The Login Process

Logging back in has a little more logic involved in it, since it's a very important part of any application as far as security goes. We'll prompt the user for a username and password, then check the hash of the password supplied against the hashed password of the user with the supplied username.

 Information Leaking

We want to give as little information away as possible if the supplied credentials fail to match a user. By simply stating "we're unable to find a user with the supplied username and password combination", we protect ourselves from malicious users attempting to figure out information about our service. If a user attempted to log in with the username "admin" and we responded with "Your password was incorrect," we've then revealed that there is indeed a username of "admin," so an unscrupulous user could try to gain access to that specific account.

Our first task is to create our `HandleSessionNew` handler, which is responsible for displaying the sign-in form. This handler also makes available the `next` parameter that we pass along in the query string to the template. If you missed it earlier, we pass on the original requested URL via a query string parameter `next` when our `RequireLogin` handler recognizes an unauthenticated user trying to access an authenticated page. We'll then redirect such users back to where they intended to go once logged in. We'll store it in the login form so that it's passed with the user credentials, and the user can be redirected on once logged in:

5_signing_out_and_in/handle_session.go (excerpt)

```go
func HandleSessionNew(w http.ResponseWriter, r *http.Request) {
    next := r.URL.Query().Get("next")
    RenderTemplate(w, r, "sessions/new", map[string]interface{}{
```

```
        "Next": next,
    })
}
```

We'll also need the corresponding login form template, which asks for a username and password and then stores the next value in a hidden input:

```
                          5_signing_out_and_in/templates/sessions/new.html (excerpt)

{{define "sessions/new"}}
<div class="row">
    <div class="col-md-6 col-md-offset-3">
        <h1>Sign In</h1>
        {{if .Error}}
        <p class="text-danger">
            {{.Error}}
        </p>
        {{end}}
        <form action="/login" method="POST">
            <div class="form-group">
                <label for="newUsername">Username</label>
                <input type="text" name="username" value="{{.User.
➡Username}}" id="newUsername" class="form-control">
            </div>
            <div class="form-group">
                <label for="password">Password</label>
                <input type="password" name="password" id="password"
➡class="form-control">
            </div>
            <input type="submit" value="Sign In" class="btn
➡btn-primary">
            <input type="hidden" name="next" value="{{.Next}}">
        </form>
    </div>
</div>
{{end}}
```

Most of this form is similar to the registration form that we've seen already; it's mainly the hidden next input, the different fields, and the fact it posts to /login that differentiates it. The error handling code is the same, for example.

The last piece of the puzzle is the handler that deals with authenticating the user credentials submitted via the form. We're yet to create all the functions this handler needs, but first let's look at what it does, then we'll fill in the missing functions afterwards:

```
5_signing_out_and_in/handle_session.go (excerpt)
func HandleSessionCreate(w http.ResponseWriter, r *http.Request, _
➥httprouter.Params){
    username := r.FormValue("username")
    password := r.FormValue("password")
    next := r.FormValue("next")

    user, err := FindUser(username, password)
    if err != nil {
        if IsValidationError(err) {
            RenderTemplate(w, r, "sessions/new", map[string]
➥interface{}{
                "Error": err,
                "User":  user,
                "Next":  next,
            })
            return
        }
        panic(err)
    }

    session := FindOrCreateSession(w, r)
    session.UserID = user.ID
    err = globalSessionStore.Save(session)
    if err != nil {
        panic(err)
    }

    if next == "" {
        next = "/"
    }

    http.Redirect(w, r, next+"?flash=Signed+in", http.StatusFound)
}
```

There are four distinct parts to this handler. At the start, we extract the values we need from the submitted form. Next up we attempt to find a user for the supplied username and password using the yet-to-be-written FindUser function. If that fails we redisplay the login form to the user with any error information we've had returned. The third part runs if we've successfully found a user from the supplied credentials, where we assign the user to the session returned from our second yet-to-be-written function FindOrCreateSession. Lastly, we redirect the user to the page they'd been intending to visit, or to the home page if there's no redirect information.

So the handler itself is straightforward, as we've managed to hide away the business logic in the function FindUser. This function is responsible for all the logic behind finding a user given the username and password, so let's look at what it needs to do. I mentioned before that we should return an error that leaks minimal information, so let's create that error first:

5_signing_out_and_in/errors.go *(excerpt)*

```
errCredentialsIncorrect = ValidationError(errors.New("We couldn't
➥find a user with the supplied username and password combination"))
```

Now we can return that error if we have a problem in FindUser:

5_signing_out_and_in/user.go *(excerpt)*

```
func FindUser(username, password string) (*User, error) {
    out := &User{
        Username: username,
    }

    existingUser, err := globalUserStore.FindByUsername(username)
    if err != nil {
        return out, err
    }
    if existingUser == nil {
        return out, errCredentialsIncorrect
    }

    if bcrypt.CompareHashAndPassword(
        []byte(existingUser.HashedPassword),
        []byte(password),
    ) != nil {
        return out, errCredentialsIncorrect
    }
```

```
      return existingUser, nil
}
```

There are three parts to this function. At the start, we create a dummy user with the username supplied. If the credentials supplied fail to match a user, the newly created out user will be returned along with an error, which will end up being displayed in the login form. It won't be used at all if the credentials are valid.

The second part of the function deals with finding a user with the supplied username. If we're unable to, we return the out user along with the new error errCredentialsIncorrect.

Lastly, if we have found a user with the supplied username, we compare the supplied password against the stored password hash using the function bcrypt.CompareHashAndPassword. This function handles the complexity of generating a hash of the supplied password with the same "cost" as the originally generated hash, and then comparing them in a secure way.

 Timing Attacks

Comparing strings naively using an x == y type comparison makes it possible over a large number of iterations to figure out how much of a match strings are. This possibly exposes important information.

If we were to compare "abc" with "afg": the program will compare the first letters and see that they are a match; then compare the second letters and see there is no match and stop. If you were to then compare "abc" with "abx," you could compare the time taken and see that since it is taking longer, the strings are a closer match. To guard against this, the bcrypt library makes use of a constant time comparison function in the crypto/subtle package, ConstantTimeCompare, where it takes the same time to compute, regardless of what the inputs are.

Now we have our FindUser function sorted, the last item left is to add the FindOrCreateSession function. This is really a helper function that looks for a session on the request, and creates it if one doesn't exist. This saves us having to write the same logic every time we want to create a session:

5_signing_out_and_in/session.go *(excerpt)*

```
func FindOrCreateSession(w http.ResponseWriter, r *http.Request)
➥*Session {
    session := RequestSession(r)
    if session == nil {
        session = NewSession(w)
    }

    return session
}
```

Congratulations! At this point, we should be able to compile and run our code, and have a fully working user system. Give it a go, register a new user, sign out, and then log in again. Try adding some errors when logging in just to make sure everything is working as expected.

Editing Your Details

The final feature to add before we can claim we have a truly solid user system is the ability for users to edit their account details. First, we'll need a new template with an edit form. We'll allow users to edit their email address and password. To update their password, they'll need to enter their current password too:

6_edit_user/templates/users/edit.html

```
{{define "users/edit"}}
<div class="row">
    <div class="col-md-6 col-md-offset-3">
        <h1>Your Details</h1>
        {{with .Error}}
        <div class="alert error">
            {{.}}
        </div>
        {{end}}
        <form action="/account" method="POST">
            <div class="form-group">
                <label for="newEmail">Email</label>
                <input type="text" name="email" value="{{.User.
➥Email}}" id="newEmail" class="form-control">
            </div>
            <h2>Change Password <small>optional</small></h2>
            <div class="form-group">
```

```
                    <label for="currentPassword">Current Password
➥</label>
                    <input type="password" name="currentPassword"
➥id="currentPassword" class="form-control">
            </div>
            <div class="form-group">
                <label for="newPassword">New Password</label>
                <input type="password" name="newPassword"
➥id="newPassword" class="form-control">
            </div>
            <input type="submit" value="Save" class="btn
➥btn-primary">
        </form>
    </div>
</div>
{{end}}
```

Now we'll add in two new handlers, the GET and POST handlers for /account, which is where account editing will live. This will be on the secureRouter in our main function, since these pages are restricted to authenticated users only. Once updated, your secureRouter code should look like so:

6_edit_user/main.go *(excerpt)*

```
// main.go
func main() {
    ⋮
    secureRouter := NewRouter()
    secureRouter.Handle("GET", "/sign-out", HandleSessionDestroy)
    secureRouter.Handle("GET", "/account", HandleUserEdit)
    secureRouter.Handle("POST", "/account", HandleUserUpdate)
    ⋮
}
```

As we've seen, the GET handler is relatively basic; it just shows the template with any values that are appropriate. In this case, the data we need to pass along is that of the currently logged in user, which we know we can get via RequestUser:

6_edit_user/handle_user.go *(excerpt)*

```
func HandleUserEdit(w http.ResponseWriter, r *http.Request, _
➥httprouter.Params) {
    user := RequestUser(r)
```

```
    RenderTemplate(w, r, "users/edit", map[string]interface{}{
        "User": user,
    })
}
```

This allows us to visit the edit page, but without the matching `HandleUserUpdate`
handler we're unable to process any of the updating:

6_edit_user/handle_user.go *(excerpt)*

```
func HandleUserUpdate(w http.ResponseWriter, r *http.Request, _
➟httprouter.Params) {
    currentUser := RequestUser(r)
    email := r.FormValue("email")
    currentPassword := r.FormValue("currentPassword")
    newPassword := r.FormValue("newPassword")

    user, err := UpdateUser(currentUser, email, currentPassword,
➟newPassword)
    if err != nil {
        if IsValidationError(err) {
            RenderTemplate(w, r, "users/edit", map[string]
➟interface{}{
                "Error": err.Error(),
                "User":  user,
            })
            return
        }
        panic(err)
    }

    err = globalUserStore.Save(*currentUser)
    if err != nil {
        panic(err)
    }

    http.Redirect(w, r, "/account?flash=User+updated", http.
➟StatusFound)
}
```

As with the `HandleSessionCreate` handler earlier in the chapter, this handler is
straightforward because we delegate the business logic to a yet-to-be-written function,
`UpdateUser`. First we retrieve the values from the submitted form; then we attempt

to update the user with those values, and display the form again if that fails. Finally, we commit the updates to the user store and redirect the user if everything is successful. it's important to note that we pass the `currentUser` variable along to the `UpdateUser` function. Since it is a pointer to the current user, the function is able to update the variable for us to save later. Let's take a look at the `UpdateUser` logic now:

6_edit_user/errors.go *(excerpt)*

```
errPasswordIncorrect    = ValidationError(errors.New("Password did
➥not match"))
```

6_edit_user/user.go *(excerpt)*

```
func UpdateUser(user *User, email, currentPassword, newPassword
➥string) (User, error) {
    out := *user
    out.Email = email

    // Check if the email exists
    existingUser, err := globalUserStore.FindByEmail(email)
    if err != nil {
        return out, err
    }
    if existingUser != nil && existingUser.ID != user.ID {
        return out, errEmailExists
    }

    // At this point, we can update the email address
    user.Email = email

    // No current password? Don't try update the password.
    if currentPassword == "" {
        return out, nil
    }

    if bcrypt.CompareHashAndPassword(
        []byte(user.HashedPassword),
        []byte(currentPassword),
    ) != nil {
        return out, errPasswordIncorrect
    }

    if newPassword == "" {
```

```
        return out, errNoPassword
    }

    if len(newPassword) < passwordLength {
        return out, errPasswordTooShort
    }

    hashedPassword, err := bcrypt.GenerateFromPassword([]byte
➥(newPassword), hashCost)
    user.HashedPassword = string(hashedPassword)
    return out, err
}
```

Let's break this function down into some logical chunks. The first task is to create a copy of the current user by de-referencing the pointer. This creates what's called a **shallow copy**, which means we won't be editing the original user (unless we were dealing with fields that were also pointers; as our users only have string fields at this point, there is no issue here). Next up, we check if a user exists with the supplied email address, and that it's not the user that we're trying to update. This means that it's fine to be updating the current user's password, but not email, for example.

Once we've confirmed that the email address isn't already taken, we assign it to the supplied user. Since this is a pointer, the calling code will see this updated email address. After that, we check to see if a password has been supplied, and, if not, there's no need to continue on with the code, as we've updated all the required fields. If there is a password, however, we'll validate it, and then update the password. We compare the supplied password against the stored user password just as we did in our FindUser function, and then we validate the new password as we did in our CreateUser function. There's nothing really new here—just a slightly different combination to how we've done it before.

You should now be able to build and run Gophr, and visit the account page to update user details. If you want to check out how the login system works, try to visit /account when you're signed out. It should redirect you to the login page, and when you login successfully, redirect you back to /account.

Summary

That's it for this chapter. At this point, we have a fully functioning user system, where users can register their accounts, manage their details, and sign out / login as they want. This is a solid skeleton for any web project, being the foundation for any web application these days — in fact, we'll see how we can wrap this up into a reusable package in a later chapter. Next up we're going to look at the fun stuff: how to upload, store, manipulate, and display images using Go.

Exercises

- Both `FileUserStore` and `SessionUserStore` contain some duplicate code, the writing to, and reading from, a file. Try and create a `FileStore` type that encapsulates this logic, and have both `FileUserStore` and `FileSessionStore` use it.

- Add different flash message types to distinguish between success, warnings, and errors. Bootstrap has different colored alert boxes for each type.

- When logging in we remember where the user intended to visit, and then redirect them once they're logged in; however, we don't do this when users register for the site. Add in this functionality using the `next` query string parameters and a hidden input field.

7

Gophr Part 4: Images

In this chapter we're going to start delving into the depths of the Gophr system. So far the work we've done has been about setting up the skeleton of a web application, which is much the same with all web apps—it's important work but hardly scintillating. Now we'll start diving into the interesting bits: uploading and displaying images.

Gophr will allow users to upload images either directly from their computer or by providing a URL for the image, which we'll then download and store. Storing image information in a flat file isn't the most performant way of keeping information, so we'll store the image meta data (rather than the images themselves) in a MySQL database and use the `database/sql` package. This will allow us to quickly and efficiently query images for displaying on various pages.

There's a lot to cover in this chapter. We'll learn about the `database/sql` package for dealing with SQL databases, using the `http` package as a client to retrieve resources from URLs, and file uploads using the `multipart` package.

The Image Type

Our first task is to define a type that will represent an image in Gophr. Images are associated with users, so as well as having its own ID, we'll also require a `userID` to associate the image with its owner. We'll also need information about the image itself, such as its filename, its location on the file system (that is, what name we've stored it as, since this may not be the same as the original filename), its file size, and when it was uploaded. Lastly, we'll allow users to add a caption that describes the image when it's uploaded:

```
                                                    1_mysql/image.go
package main

import "time"

type Image struct{
    ID          string
    UserID      string
    Name        string
    Location    string
    Size        int64
    CreatedAt   time.Time
    Description string
}
```

This simple data structure provides all the information we need to know about an image. When we upload an image, we'll copy it into a directory under the `data` directory and rename it to a filename based on the image ID. By doing this we'll avoid any clashes with the filename, as there's bound to be more than one **IMG_0001.jpg** uploaded (indeed, you can replace 0001 with almost any number and this will likely be true).

ImageStore Interface

As with our previous data types, `User` and `Session`, a store is necessary to place our `Image` data. Implementing this store as an interface is logical as well, since you may well decide that MySQL isn't suitable and start storing images in Riak or MongoDB, or printed out on paper cards and stored in a filing cabinet at your office.

Regardless of the underlying store, having an interface allows for future flexibility, so we'll be doing that again.

When it comes to the actions we want to perform on our `ImageStore` interface, they are limited to the types of displays we'll be providing on the Gophr site. For the moment, the front page will be displaying a list of recently uploaded images, which maps to a `FindAll` method that returns the latest records sorted by `CreatedAt`. We'll also allow a view of a user's images, so following the same idea except filtered to just one user, `FindAllByUser`. Lastly we'll require the ability to both find and save a single image. This leaves us with an interface with four methods:

```
                                                      1_mysql/image.go

package main

type ImageStore interface{
    Save(image *Image) error
    Find(id string) (*Image, error)
    FindAll(offset int) ([]Image, error)
    FindAllByUser(user *User, offset int) ([]Image, error)
}
```

You'll see that the `FindAll` and `FindAllByUser` methods take an `int` named `offset`. This allows you to page through results, so you're not limited to just the latest results.

Getting My(SQL) Groove On

Now's the time to make sure that we have access to a MySQL database. If you're a seasoned web developer, chances are that you have a preferred way of doing this, so I'll avoid prescribing a single way to do it. You can install it with whatever package manager you like, download directly from the website, or use a third-party bundle; just make sure that you have a MySQL database, the access information, and the permission to create databases.

If you don't have MySQL installed, you can download the free community edition directly from the MySQL website.[1] Follow the instructions on the website to get MySQL up and running—in fact, go do that now.

---

[1] http://dev.mysql.com/downloads/mysql/

For the creation of databases and table schemas, I'll be using MySQL Workbench,[2] a cross-platform tool provided by the MySQL team. This is by no means the only—or best—tool on the market; you're welcome to use whatever tool you're comfortable with (such as the MySQL command line), but just be aware it will look different to what appears on these pages..

MySQL Requirements

To start off, we'll create a new database for Gophr. We're going to conveniently name it gophr, and the command to do this is:

```
CREATE DATABASE gophr;
```

It should look like Figure 7.1.

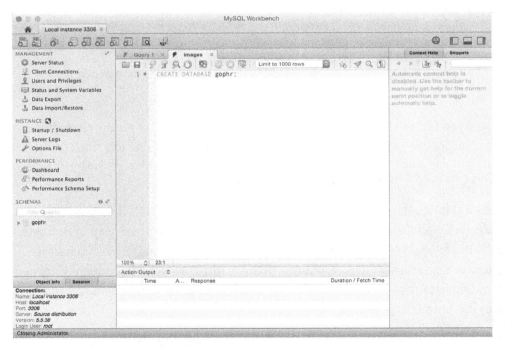

Figure 7.1. Creating a database

Next we run USE gopher; to ensure that we're working with the Gophr database from here on out.

---

[2] http://dev.mysql.com/downloads/workbench/

Now we define our one and only table for the moment, our `images` table. This table will mirror the structure we've defined for our `Image` type in Go. The main point of interest is that we're defining an index on the `user_id` column. This will allow us to look up a user's images in an efficient manner:

```
CREATE TABLE `images` (
  `id` varchar(255) NOT NULL DEFAULT '',
  `user_id` varchar(255) NOT NULL,
  `name` varchar(255) NOT NULL DEFAULT '',
  `location` varchar(255) NOT NULL DEFAULT '',
  `description` text NOT NULL,
  `size` int(11) NOT NULL,
  `created_at` datetime NOT NULL,
  PRIMARY KEY (`id`),
  KEY `user_id_idx` (`user_id`)
) ENGINE=InnoDB DEFAULT CHARSET=utf8;
```

This should look something like Figure 7.2.

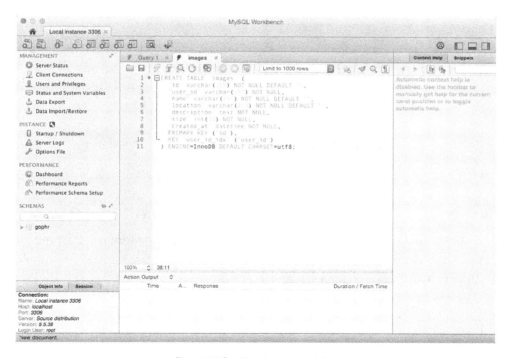

Figure 7.2. Creating the `images` table

Connecting to Databases

Now we have a database that's running, we'll look at how Go lets us access databases in general. Unlike a lot of languages, Go takes an approach that abstracts away the specific database from the library used to access it. It provides a `database/sql` library that can be used to access most SQL databases. By default, it has no implementations, just a standard API for access and querying. For an actual implementation you still require a third-party library, but instead of calling and using it, you only need ensure it's imported. Once imported, the library will register itself with `database/sql`, and then you can use the `database/sql` package directly.

Since we're using MySQL, we'll need a MySQL package. We're going to use the library `github.com/go-sql-driver/mysql` for Gophr, which provides a stable MySQL client implementation in pure Go.

To start, you should use the `go get` tool to retrieve the package:

```
go get github.com/go-sql-driver/mysql
```

Now we can use the package in our code. If you just import the package in the conventional way, you'll receive errors along the lines of `imported and not used: 'github.com/go-sql-driver/mysql'`. To get around this, use the blank identifier to say "import this code, but we're not going to use it right here":

```
                                               1_mysql/mysql.go (excerpt)

package main

import _ "github.com/go-sql-driver/mysql"
```

This allows the package to be included in the code and therefore run its `func init()`, in which it registers itself with the `database/sql` package as the code to handle any `mysql` connections.

Next up we're going to create a global MySQL database to use. The `database/sql` package has an `Open` function that takes the name of the database type, and a **Data Source Name** (or `dsn`) that provides all the information required to connect to the database, including authentication and database name information. This function alsoreturns a pointer to an instance of `sql.DB`. Note that this isn't a single connection to a database; the `database/sql` package will actually maintain a pool of connections, and reuse connections when it can. This means you can skip having to think too hard about managing or reusing connections, as for most use cases it will just work:

1_mysql/mysql.go (excerpt)

```go
import (
    "database/sql"

    _ "github.com/go-sql-driver/mysql"
)

var globalMySQLDB *sql.DB

func init() {
    db, err := NewMySQLDB("root:root@tcp(127.0.0.1:3306)/gophr")
    if err != nil {
        panic(err)
    }
    globalMySQLDB = db
}

func NewMySQLDB(dsn string) (*sql.DB, error) {
    db, err := sql.Open("mysql", dsn+"?parseTime=true")
    if err != nil {
        return nil, err
    }

    return db, db.Ping()
}
```

Here you can see there are two separate chunks of code. The first is calling NewMySQLDB with a dsn, checking for errors and assigning the sql.DB instance to a variable globalMySQLDB. The second chunk is the function NewMySQLDB, which is responsible for opening the database connection and returning it. Note that we also call db.Ping() at the end. This method verifies that a connection is alive, or establishes one if none exist yet. By doing this now, we avoid a situation later where any errors in connecting to the database would occur only when the first real query was run, which would be in response to a user request. I think we can all agree that we'd rather see errors when starting the app than let a user see a "database not found" error!

The dsn that we're using provides all the information to connect to the gophr database in our MySQL server. You may need to change some of these values to match your server's configuration, but the general idea is {username}:{password}@tcp({address}:{port})/{database_name}. We're connecting to our local server, which is available at 127.0.0.1.

At this point you should be able to compile your code and run it without seeing any errors. If you receive an error, it's most likely to do with your dsn value or your MySQL server running incorrectly.

Creating `ImageStore`

Our next task is to create an implementation of ImageStore that uses MySQL to retrieve and save images. We'll call it DBImageStore, and define it very simply as a struct that has a field db *sql.DB. We'll also define a function NewDBImageStore that returns an instance with the db field set to the globalMySQLDB instance, which we created earlier in the chapter. Lastly, we can create a new globalImageStore instance of type ImageStore, just like we did with the UserStore and SessionStore interfaces:

```
                                    2_db_image_store/image_store.go (excerpt)

import "database/sql"

var globalImageStore ImageStore

type DBImageStore struct{
    db *sql.DB
}

func NewDBImageStore() ImageStore {
    return &DBImageStore{
        db: globalMySQLDB,
    }
}
```

Note that we're yet to initialise globalImageStore, and I'll explain why a little later on. For now, we'll continue to define the methods required to implement the ImageStore interface.

Implementing ImageStore in DBImageStore

There are four methods to implement: one to save images and three to find images. We'll start with the save method.

Save

We're going to use the `Exec(query string, args ...interface{})` method on our `sql.DB` instance. This method takes a query string representing the SQL you want to run, using the `?` character for replacement variables. After the query string, we'll pass the values to be used for replacement. If our query string was `DELETE FROM images WHERE id = ?`, we'd have to pass one value after this, the value of the ID we wanted to delete. The `database/sql` package passes this off to the `mysql` package to correctly escape and insert the value into the query. If you passed in an ID of "abc123", the final query would be `DELETE FROM images WHERE id = 'abc123'`. This placeholder replacement allows for the secure escaping of values, so you can be assured you're safe from common SQL injection techniques.

For our save method, we're going to use the `REPLACE INTO` statement. This statement allows us to handle both an insert and an update in one go. If no record exists with a matching primary key a new one will be created, but if a record exists it will be deleted before this row is added. Now there's no need to worry about whether or not an image has been previously created—we can just save it:

2_db_image_store/image_store.go *(excerpt)*

```
func (store *DBImageStore) Save(image *Image) error {
    _, err := store.db.Exec(
        `
        REPLACE INTO images
            (id, user_id, name, location, description, size,
➥created_at)
        VALUES
            (?, ?, ?, ?, ?, ?, ?)
        `,
        image.ID,
        image.UserID,
        image.Name,
        image.Location,
        image.Description,
        image.Size,
        image.CreatedAt,
```

```
        )
        return err
}
```

As you can see, the query is using `REPLACE INTO` to set all the columns on the `images` table with all the fields from the `Image` type. Since there are seven fields to be added, we have seven placeholder values in the query and seven additional arguments to the `Exec` method with the values to be used.

Find

Next up, we'll look at the finder methods. We'll start with the `Find` method, which takes an image ID and returns a single image. Instead of the `Exec` method, we'll be using the `QueryRow` method. This method should be used when you want to know about the results of a query and you think only one row will be returned. A sister method, `Query`, will be used in the `FindAll` and `FindAllByUser` methods when we expect more than one result:

2_db_image_store/image_store.go (excerpt)

```
func (store *DBImageStore) Find(id string) (*Image, error) {
    row := store.db.QueryRow(
        `
        SELECT id, user_id, name, location, description, size,
➥created_at
        FROM images
        WHERE id = ?`,
        id,
    )

    image := Image{}
    err := row.Scan(
        &image.ID,
        &image.UserID,
        &image.Name,
        &image.Location,
        &image.Description,
        &image.Size,
        &image.CreatedAt,
```

```
    )
    return &image, err
}
```

This function can be broken down into two parts: the querying of the database and the unmarshalling of results into an instance of `Image`. `QueryRow` and `Query` are just like `Exec` in that they take a query with placeholder markers, followed by the values to be escaped and inserted into the markers. In this case, we're asking for the values from a single image and passing in the image ID as a replacement value. Note that we receive no error value back as a result of the `QueryRow` method. This is because the query itself is only run when we want to scan the results into a variable.

The `Scan` method on the row returned is responsible for applying the values returned from the database into variables. If any problems occur, the method will return an error. This could be a problem with the query itself, or a mismatch with the values you're trying to scan. If the database has returned an integer, you cannot scan it into a string variable and Go will return an error describing this problem.

In our case, we've created a new `Image` and are passing pointers to the appropriate columns in the row from the database. The order of values passed into `Scan` needs to be the same as the order of columns in the query. Most problems when dealing with the database arise as a result of a scan error, either a type mismatch or incorrect column ordering.

 Null Values

Go won't handle scanning a null MySQL value into a string or number type. To get around this, you can either use a pointer to a type or have a look at the NullXXX types in the database/sql package.[3] These types allow you to scan in a value that can be null, but to achieve the non-null value you have to call a method `Value` on the type, which can introduce complexity.

FindAll

The `FindAll` method is slightly different because it expects to return an array of images rather than just the one. This means we have to use `Query` method instead

---

[3] http://golang.org/pkg/database/sql/#pkg-index

of the `QueryRow` method. `Query` returns an `sql.Rows` type and an error. We'll use the `sql.Rows` to iterate over the results and scan them into images:

```go
const pageSize = 25

⋮

func (store *DBImageStore) FindAll(offset int) ([]Image, error) {
    rows, err := store.db.Query(
        `
        SELECT id, user_id, name, location, description, size,
➥created_at
        FROM images
        ORDER BY created_at DESC
        LIMIT ?
        OFFSET ?
        `,
        pageSize,
        offset,
    )
    if err != nil {
        return nil, err
    }

    images := []Image{}
    for rows.Next() {
        image := Image{}
        err := rows.Scan(
            &image.ID,
            &image.UserID,
            &image.Name,
            &image.Location,
            &image.Description,
            &image.Size,
            &image.CreatedAt,
        )
        if err != nil {
            return nil, err
        }

        images = append(images, image)
    }
```

```
    return images, nil
}
```

As with `Find`, this method is broken down into type areas—firstly querying the database, then dealing with the results. Our query is a little more complicated than before. We're selecting the same columns, but instead of the `WHERE` clause we're just asking for all values, ordered by their creation date with the newest first. We also limit the results to 25 values, stored in the constant `pageSize`, and start with the results at an offset. If we pass in an offset of `0`, we'll receive the first 25 results, whereas an offset of `25` would get us the second 25 results.

Since `Query` returns an error, too, we need to check that error for problems. Once we've done that we create the array of images to return, then loop through the results with the `rows.Next` method. This method will return true as long as there are rows that can be scanned. Once `rows.Next` returns false, the `for` loop will stop and we'll return the images. Inside the `for` loop, we scan the values into a new `Image` just like we did in the `Find` method; then we append the image to the array of images we'll be returning.

FindAllByUser

Last of all, we have the `FindAllByUser` method, which is very similar to `FindAll`. Almost all the code is the same; the only difference is that we'll add a `WHERE` clause to limit the images to just those with the supplied user's ID:

2_db_image_store/image_store.go (excerpt)

```
func (store *DBImageStore) FindAllByUser(user *User, offset int)
➡([]Image, error) {
    rows, err := store.db.Query(
        `
        SELECT id, user_id, name, location, description, size,
➡created_at
        FROM images
        WHERE user_id = ?
        ORDER BY created_at DESC
        LIMIT ?
        OFFSET ?`,
        user.ID,
        pageSize,
```

```
        offset,
    )
    if err != nil {
        return nil, err
    }

    images := []Image{}
    for rows.Next() {
        image := Image{}
        err := rows.Scan(
            &image.ID,
            &image.UserID,
            &image.Name,
            &image.Location,
            &image.Description,
            &image.Size,
            &image.CreatedAt,
        )
        if err != nil {
            return nil, err
        }

        images = append(images, image)
    }

    return images, nil
}
```

There you have it. We've now created all the methods required to implement the `ImageStore` interface. The only task that's left is to assign a new `DBImageStore` to our `globalImageStore` variable. Previously we've done this for `globalUserStore`, `globalSessionStore`, and `globalMySQLDB` by creating a new variable inside an `init` method in each of the files. This has worked so far because there are no dependencies on other variables. That's no longer the case, as the `NewDBImageStore` creates a `DBImageStore` with the `globalMySQLDB` value assigned to the `db` field. The problem with this is that if we created this inside the `init` function in image_store.go, the chances are that `globalMySQLDB` would still be `nil`, since the `init` function of mysql.go has yet to run. This is obviously not what we're trying to achieve, so we need to approach it a little differently. We'll move all the creation of global variables inside the `init` function into **main.go**, and remember to remove the `init` code from **user_store.go**, **session_store.go**, and **mysql.go**:

```
                                              2_db_image_store/main.go (excerpt)

func init(){
    // Assign a user store
    store, err := NewFileUserStore("./data/users.json")
    if err != nil {
        panic(fmt.Errorf("Error creating user store: %s", err))
    }
    globalUserStore = store

    // Assign a session store
    sessionStore, err := NewFileSessionStore("./data/sessions.json")
    if err != nil {
        panic(fmt.Errorf("Error creating session store: %s", err))
    }
    globalSessionStore = sessionStore

    // Assign a sql database
    db, err := NewMySQLDB("root:root@tcp(127.0.0.1:3306)/gophr")
    if err != nil {
        panic(err)
    }
    globalMySQLDB = db

    // Assign an image store
    globalImageStore = NewDBImageStore()
}
```

 Managing Dependencies in the Real World

Managing dependencies is one of the harder parts of dealing with real-life applications. Sometimes you can get by with global values, sometimes you can't. It's beyond the scope of this book, and the example application, to cover the technical issues of dealing with dependencies. Gophr will run fine by passing around global values, but if Gophr gains some traction and suddenly you're dealing with millions of visitors a day, you may find that maintaining your app will become difficult.

Uploading Images

Now it's time for the fun stuff. We're going to enable our users to upload their images to Gophr. We can provide them with two easy methods: file uploads from their computer, and uploads from an image URL.

The first job is to add a couple of route handlers. We'll need to show the image upload form and handle the submission, so a GET and POST route for /images/new will work. Add this inside the main function in **main.go**:

```
3_uploading_images/main.go (excerpt)

secureRouter.Handle("GET", "/images/new", HandleImageNew)
secureRouter.Handle("POST", "/images/new", HandleImageCreate)
```

Next up are the handler functions for displaying and processing the image upload form, as well as the form itself. All that's required for the form is an input for the file upload and file URL, along with a description box. Following our naming convention, we'll place the template in images/new:

```
3_uploading_images/templates/images/new.html

{{define "images/new"}}
<div class="row">
    <div class="col-md-6 col-md-offset-3">
        <h1>Add An Image</h1>
        {{if .Error}}
        <p class="text-danger">
            {{.Error}}
        </p>
        {{end}}
        <form action="/images/new" method="POST" enctype="multipart/
➡form-data">
            <div class="form-group">
                <label for="imageUrl">Upload from URL</label>
                <input type="text" name="url" id="imageUrl" value=
➡"{{.ImageUrl}}" class="form-control">
            </div>
            <div class="form-group">
                <label for="imageUpload">Upload from file</label>
                <input type="file" name="file" id="imageUpload"
➡class="form-control">
            </div>
            <div class="form-group">
                <label for="description">Description</label>
                <textarea name="description" id="description" class=
➡"form-control">{{.Image.Description}}</textarea>
            </div>
            <input type="submit" value="Add" class="btn
➡btn-primary">
```

```
        </form>
    </div>
</div>
{{end}}
```

Now we'll create the two handler functions that both display and process the form. Like our previous GET handlers, HandleImageNew is very simple and just displays the form:

3_uploading_images/handle_image.go (excerpt)

```
func HandleImageNew(w http.ResponseWriter, r *http.Request, _
➥httprouter.Params) {
    RenderTemplate(w, r, "images/new", nil)
}
```

It's only when we hit HandleImageCreate that it all starts to get a bit interesting. Since we're actually processing an image from one of two sources, we'll use this handler to decide which type of image upload we're going to deal with, then pass the processing off to a handler that just deals with the one responsibility—creating an image from a file or creating an image from a remote URL:

3_uploading_images/handle_image.go (excerpt)

```
func HandleImageCreate(w http.ResponseWriter, r *http.Request, _
➥httprouter.Params) {
    if r.FormValue("url") != "" {
        HandleImageCreateFromURL(w, r)
        return
    }

    HandleImageCreateFromFile(w, r)
}
```

We check to see whether we've received a URL in the posted form and if so, we pass processing off to the HandleImageCreateFromURL function; otherwise we fall back to HandleImageCreateFromFile. This is a nice way to separate out the responsibilities, and since each of those handlers could be used on their own, in the future we could have two completely separate processes for uploading files and just use the handler functions directly.

Creating Images from a URL

Creating an image from a URL is surprisingly easy with Go. So far we've been using the `http` package as a server rather than as a client, meaning we are writing the app that handles the requests and dishes out responses to a client. When it comes to obtaining content from a remote URL, the roles reverse and we become the client. We'll make a request to the remote URL for its content, and then consume the response.

Since the logic for retrieving and dealing with the URL isn't really specific to the handler so much as a process that could be used in a variety of ways, we'll move that code into a method on the `Image` type, and just use the handler to orchestrate the request and response:

3_uploading_images/handle_image.go (excerpt)

```go
func HandleImageCreateFromURL(w http.ResponseWriter, r *http.
➥Request) {
    user := RequestUser(r)

    image := NewImage(user)
    image.Description = r.FormValue("description")

    err := image.CreateFromURL(r.FormValue("url"))

    if err != nil {
        if IsValidationError(err) {
            RenderTemplate(w, r, "images/new", map[string]
➥interface{}{
                "Error":    err,
                "ImageURL": r.FormValue("url"),
                "Image":    image,
            })
            return
        }
        panic(err)
    }
}
```

```
    http.Redirect(w, r, "/?flash=Image+Uploaded+Successfully", http.
➥StatusFound)
}
```

Breaking the handler down, we start by retrieving the user for this request and creating an image that belongs to them. After adding the description that was posted with the request, we call the `CreateFromURL` method along with the URL that was posted. This method will handle all the complexity of downloading the remote resource, so we only have to deal with a possible error or redirecting the user. If we do receive an error, we display the page again with the error; otherwise the upload was fine so we redirect to the home page with a "success" message.

All the complexity lies inside the `CreateFromURL` method on the `Image` type. This method is the most complex functionality we've seen so far, so I'll describe what it's going to do ahead of time so that you have some understanding of the code as you go through it. First, we're going to retrieve the image from the URL and check that we've received a valid response. After that we'll check it's a valid image type, and then save it to our server. Last, we'll save the updated `Image` with the information it requires:

3_uploading_images/errors.go (excerpt)

```
var (
    ⋮

    // Image Manipulation Errors
    errInvalidImageType = ValidationError(errors.New("Please upload
➥only jpeg, gif or png images"))
    errNoImage          = ValidationError(errors.New("Please select
➥an image to upload"))
    errImageURLInvalid = ValidationError(errors.New("Couldn't
➥download image from the URL you provided"))
)
```

3_uploading_images/image.go (excerpt)

```
const imageIDLength = 10

func NewImage(user *User) *Image{
    return &Image{
        ID:          GenerateID("img", imageIDLength),
```

```go
        UserID:    user.ID,
        CreatedAt: time.Now(),
    }
}

// A map of accepted mime types and their file extension
var mimeExtensions = map[string]string{
    "image/png":  ".png",
    "image/jpeg": ".jpg",
    "image/gif":  ".gif",
}

func (image *Image) CreateFromURL(imageURL string) error {
    // Get the response from the URL
    response, err := http.Get(imageURL)
    if err != nil {
        return err
    }

    // Make sure we have a response
    if response.StatusCode != http.StatusOK {
        return errImageURLInvalid
    }

    defer response.Body.Close()

    // Ascertain the type of file we downloaded
    mimeType, _, err := mime.ParseMediaType(response.Header.Get
➡("Content-Type"))
    if err != nil {
        return errInvalidImageType
    }

    // Get an extension for the file
    ext, valid := mimeExtensions[mimeType]
    if !valid {
        return errInvalidImageType
    }

    // Get a name from the URL
    image.Name = filepath.Base(imageURL)
    image.Location = image.ID + ext

    // Open a file at target location
    savedFile, err := os.Create("./data/images/" + image.Location)
```

```
    if err != nil {
        return err
    }
    defer savedFile.Close()

    // Copy the entire response to the output flie
    size, err := io.Copy(savedFile, response.Body)
    if err != nil {
        return err
    }
    // The returned value from io.Copy is the number of bytes copied
    image.Size = size

    // Save our image to the store
    return globalImageStore.Save(image)
}
```

Okay, so our first undertaking was to create a lookup map of content types to extensions. We'll use this for two reasons: to ensure we only deal with URLs that return images (as there's no point in saving an HTML file as an image) and to name our file. While a lot of URLs correctly represent an image with an extension (such as `http://example.com/image.gif`), it's perfectly valid to find an image at a URL with no file extension (such as `http://example.com/image/`), or even have an extension that doesn't match the content type (such as returning a PNG even though the URL says `.jpg`). Because we can't assume we'll receive a valid file extension, we use the content type map to provide one for us.

The first part of the `CreateFromURL` method requests the URL via `http.Get` and checks that we received a `200 OK` response. `http.Get` is a shortcut helper that the `http` package provides. After we've made sure the response is okay, we defer a call to close the body of the response. This means that we don't have to worry about closing the bodu later in every early return from the function, or before the very end. If a response body is read but not closed, it will not close the connection (part of `http.Transport`). Unclosed connections cannot be reused and you may run into issues with performance, open file descriptors, or a variety of other issues.

 ### More Advanced Requests

For a lot of requests the `http.Get` and `http.Post` functions are all you need, but if you want more control over the request you're making, such as to add headers or authentication, you can do that too. `http.Get` effectively creates a new `http.Request` and asks a default `http.Client` provided by the `http` package to make the request over the default `http.Transport`. It could be rewritten like this:

```
// Create a new http.Client, or use http.DefaultClient
// The default http.Transport will be used if you don't
// provide one
client := http.Client{}

// Create a new GET http.Request, with no body data
request := http.NewRequest("GET", imageURL, nil)

// You could add something to the request here

// Get the response, the same values are returned
// from http.Get
response, err := client.Do(request)
```

Once we know we have a valid response from the URL, we check to ensure we can deal with the type of response. First up we process the `Content-Type` header of the response using the `mime` package function `ParseMediaType`. This gives us a media type string that we use to look up the extension from our extension map. This performs two tasks for us: it gives us a variable `ext`, which is the extension to be used, and a variable `valid`, which is only true if the value existed in the map. A false value here means that we're not cool with the type of response this is, and should bail out with an `errInvalidImageType`.

After we've validated that the response is okay, it's all smooth sailing. We just need to get the information to save, and copy the response to the file system. We obtain the name of the file via the `filepath` package's `Base` function, which returns the basename from the URL. The **basename** is the last segment of the URL, so `http://example.com/image.jpg` would be `image.jpg` and `http://example.com/image/` would be `image`. The location of the image, which is where we store it on our server, is a combination of the image's ID and the extension, so an image ID of `img_abc123` might have a location of **img_abc123.png**. Once we know the final destination we open a new file at that location, in this case in the directory **./data/images**, and defer closing the body until the end of the function.

The last task is to use the io package to copy the contents of the response body to the newly created file. Once this is done, the response is now a file on our local file system. The io.Copy function returns an int representing the bytes copied, which will equal the size of our file, so we update the image before finally saving the image with the globalImageStore.

Creating Images from a File

The process of dealing with an uploaded file is a lot simpler. We can access the file and its information via the FormFile method on an http.Request. Like in our HandleImageCreateFromURL function, we'll keep the HandleImageCreateFromFile function that orchestrates the request and response, and move the heavy lifting into a method on Image:

```
                                    3_uploading_images/handle_image.go (excerpt)
func HandleImageCreateFromFile(w http.ResponseWriter, r *http.
➥Request) {

    user := RequestUser(r)
    image := NewImage(user)
    image.Description = r.FormValue("description")

    file, headers, err := r.FormFile("file")

    // No file was uploaded.
    if file == nil {
        RenderTemplate(w, r, "images/new", map[string]interface{}{
            "Error": errNoImage,
            "Image": image,
        })
        return
    }

    // A file was uploaded, but an error occurred
    if err != nil {
        panic(err)
    }

    defer file.Close()

    err = image.CreateFromFile(file, headers)
    if err != nil {
```

```
        RenderTemplate(w, r, "images/new", map[string]interface{}{
            "Error": err,
            "Image": image,
        })
        return
    }

    http.Redirect(w, r, "/?flash=Image+Uploaded+Successfully",
➥http.StatusFound)
}
```

Like before, we get the user from the request and create an image with some of the posted information. Next up, we ask for the file information for our file. `FormFile` returns three values: a `multipart.File` representing the file itself, a `multipart.File-Header` instance representing information about the file, and an error. If the file is `nil`, then no file was uploaded, so we immediately check this and return with an error `errNoImage` response. If we do have a file, we defer a call to close it and call `CreateFromFile` on the image. Any error in `CreateFromFile` will cause us to display an error page, otherwise we redirect to the home page with a "success" message.

The `CreateFromFile` method on `Image` is a lot simpler than `CreateFromURL` for one main reason: we already have the contents of the image as they were uploaded with the request. We just need to copy the file into place and update the image with the required information:

3_uploading_images/image.go (excerpt)

```
func (image *Image) CreateFromFile(file multipart.File, headers
➥*multipart.FileHeader) error {

    // Move our file to an appropriate place, with an appropriate
➥name
    image.Name = headers.Filename
    image.Location = image.ID + filepath.Ext(image.Name)

    // Open a file at the target location
    savedFile, err := os.Create("./data/images/" + image.Location)
    if err != nil {
        return err
    }

    defer savedFile.Close()
```

```
    // Copy the uploaded file to the target location
    size, err := io.Copy(savedFile, file)
    if err != nil {
        return err
    }
    image.Size = size

    // Save the image to the database
    return globalImageStore.Save(image)
}
```

The majority of this method looks the same as the `CreateFromURL` method, so we'll just focus on the first few lines. We use the file headers to provide the name of the file, and also to extract the file extension using `filepath.Ext`. After that we set the location based on the image ID and extension, copy the files and save the image – just like before.

Before you compile your code we'll add in a link to the upload page, since we can't expect our users to know it. Open up **templates/layout.html** and add in a link above `{{if .CurrentUser}}`:

```
<a href='/images/new' class='btn btn-primary'>Add Image</a>
```

At this point, you should be able to compile your code and upload files from both your computer and remote URLs! You should do this right now to check that everything is working. If all is successful, you'll see the images start to appear in the `./data/images` directory. You can also view your MySQL database and see the data being stored there. The only place where you won't see anything displayed is Gophr, because we're yet to write anything to display there—that's next.

Displaying Images

The last and—some might say—most important part of having images on your image site is to actually display them. We should do that now.

There are going to be three pages that handle displaying of images:

▢ The *home page*, which will show the latest images from across the site.

- The *image* page, which shows just a single image along with information about it.
- The *user* page, which displays just the images from a single user.

Since the home page and user page will share a bit of code, we'll create a new template `images/index` that uses an array of images, and use it in both the `index/home` and `users/show` templates:

```
                                    4_displaying_images/templates/index/home.html

{{define "index/home"}}
    {{template "images/index" .}}
{{end}}
```

```
                                    4_displaying_images/templates/images/home.html

{{define "images/index"}}
    <div class="row">
    {{if .Images}}
        {{range .Images}}
            <div class="col-xs-12 col-sm-6 col-md-3">
                <a href="{{.ShowRoute}}" class="thumbnail">
                    <img src="{{.StaticRoute}}">
                </a>
            </div>
        {{end}}
    {{else}}
    <h2>No Images Yet</h2>
    <a href='/images/new'>Why not upload one?</a>
    {{end}}
    </div>
{{end}}
```

You'll see that we iterate over an array of images, each time displaying an image inside a link. There are two methods being called on each image: `ShowRoute` and `StaticRoute`. These are methods we'll add to the `Image` type that returns the route for the image. The `ShowRoute` is the route to that image's own page, while the `StaticRoute` is the route to the image itself, which is why it's used as the `src` of the `img` tag. Let's add them now:

```
                                         4_displaying_images/image.go

func (image *Image) StaticRoute() string {
    return "/im/" + image.Location
}
func (image *Image) ShowRoute() string {
    return "/image/" + image.ID
}
```

You'll see that we're using two slightly different routes here. A shortened
/im/img_xxxx for the actual raw image file, and /image/img_xxxxx for the page
that shows the single image on Gophr. We'll add the handlers and functionality for
showing a single image shortly; for now we'll just add a handler for the raw image.

Handling the raw image files is easily dealt with by the ServeFiles method of our
routers. We serve files by listening on /im/*filepath and provide a directory to
serve from: data/images. We'll add it to the main router instance rather than secureRouter, since there's no need to be logged in to view the files:

```
                                    4_displaying_images/main.go (excerpt)

    router.ServeFiles(
        "/im/*filepath",
        http.Dir("data/images/"),
    )
```

Showing the Front Page Images

Now that we're ready to display the home page images, all we have to do is add in
an array of images to the data sent to the template. Let's replace our HandleFHome
function:

```
                                 4_displaying_images/handle_index.go

func HandleHome(w http.ResponseWriter, r *http.Request) {
    images, err := globalImageStore.FindAll(0)
    if err != nil {
        panic(err)
    }
    RenderTemplate(w, r, "index/home", map[string]interface{}{
```

```
        "Images": images,
    })
}
```

The images for the front page are found by calling `globalImageStore.FindAll(0)`. We can then assign them as the key `Images` in the data that we send through to the templates. If you compile your code now, you'll see the front page displaying all the images you've uploaded like in Figure 7.3.

Figure 7.3. Displaying our front page images

Showing a Single Image

Now we'll add a handler for a single image. We saw earlier that the route for these pages is `/image/img_xxxx`. Let's add that handler to the `router` in `main.go`. You'll notice we're using a named replacement value `:imageID`. This allows us to look up whatever value is eventually used in the URL by that name:

```
router.Handle("GET", "/image/:imageID", HandleImageShow)
```

The `HandleImageShow` function has two roles—get the image and retrieve the image's user:

```
func HandleImageShow(w http.ResponseWriter, r *http.Request, params
➥httprouter.Params) {
    image, err := globalImageStore.Find(params.ByName("imageID"))
    if err != nil {
        panic(err)
    }

    // 404
    if image == nil {
        http.NotFound(w, r)
        return
    }

    user, err := globalUserStore.Find(image.UserID)
    if err != nil {
        panic(err)
    }

    if user == nil {
        panic(fmt.Errorf("Could not find user %s", image.UserID))
    }

    RenderTemplate(w, r, "images/show", map[string]interface{}{
        "Image": image,
        "User":  user,
    })

}
```

You'll see we obtain the image name from the `params` variable, which we haven't been assigning previously. This is an instance of `httprouter.Params`, which lets us look up values provided in the URL by the name we assign to them when attaching routes. Since we assigned a name of `:imageID`, we can look this up and expect to find the image ID. If no image is found we return a 404; otherwise we retrieve the user that belongs to the image and render `images/show`. Now we'll create the matching template:

4_displaying_images/templates/images/show.html

```
{{define "images/show"}}
<div class="row">
    <div class="col-md-8 col-xd-12">
        <img src="{{.Image.StaticRoute}}" class="img-rounded" style=
➥"max-width: 100%" alt="{{.Image.Description}}">
    </div>
    <div class="col-md-4 col-xs-12">
        <div class="media">
            <a href="{{.User.ImagesRoute}}" class="pull-left">
                <img src="{{.User.AvatarURL}}" alt="{{.User.
➥Username}}">
            </a>
            <div class="media-body">
                <h3 class="media-heading">{{.User.Username}}</h3>
                <p>{{.Image.Description}}</p>
            </div>
        </div>
    </div>
</div>
{{end}}
```

There are two method calls in this template that are yet to exist. The first is to `.User.ImagesRoute`, which is a function that returns the route to the page for just that user's images. These routes will look like `/user/usr_xxxxx`. The second is to `.User.AvatarURL`, which is a function that will return a URL for a user's avatar image. Since we have no image for our users, we'll provide a URL to the popular Gravatar service,[4] which creates a link based on the MD5 hash of a user's email address. This is a good way to access avatars for some users, even when they haven't uploaded one to your service:

4_displaying_images/user.go *(excerpt)*

```
import (
    "crypto/md5"
    "io"
    "fmt"
```

---

[4] https://en.gravatar.com/

```
)

func (user *User) AvatarURL() string {
    return fmt.Sprintf(
        "//www.gravatar.com/avatar/%x",
        md5.Sum([]byte(user.Email)),
    )
}

func (user *User) ImagesRoute() string {
    return "/user/" + user.ID
}
```

The ImagesRoute method is self-explanatory so we'll focus on the AvatarURL
method. It calculates an MD5 sum using the crypto/md5 package that's part of the
Go standard library. We provide the user's email address as a byte array and append
the resulting hash to a Gravatar URL that will return an avatar image associated
with the user's email address. If the user decides against having a Gravatar, they'll
receive a dynamically generated default image.

If you now compile and view your code, you'll be able to click through to an image
from the front page and see the show image page in all its glory, as seen in Figure 7.4.

Figure 7.4. An example of the show image page

Showing a User's Images Only

Our final task is to implement the page that shows only a user's images. We've already written the majority of the code needed to run this—from the method on our ImageStore instance through to the partial template used on the front page. We just have to add a route, handler, and template to the mix.

In **main.go** we can add a route to handle the user images page that we linked to at /user/usr_xxxx. Just like with the show image page, we'll use a named replacement value in the URL as the user ID:

4_displaying_images/main.go *(excerpt)*

```
router.Handle("GET", "/user/:userID", HandleUserShow)
```

The HandleUserShow method needs to get the user and the latest images that belong to the user. Getting the user is the responsibility of the globalUserStore.Find while the images will be found by globalUserStore.FindAllByUser:

```
                              4_displaying_images/handle_user.go (excerpt)

func HandleUserShow(w http.ResponseWriter, r *http.Request, params
➥httprouter.Params) {
    user, err := globalUserStore.Find(params.ByName("userID"))
    if err != nil {
        panic(err)
    }

    // 404
    if user == nil {
        http.NotFound(w, r)
        return
    }

    images, err := globalImageStore.FindAllByUser(user, 0)
    if err != nil {
        panic(err)
    }

    RenderTemplate(w, r, "users/show", map[string]interface{}{
        "Images": images,
        "User":   user,
    })
}
```

Nothing in the `HandleUserShow` function is unusual at this point, so we now write the `users/show` template. This template will display some information about the user similar to the `images/show` template, and then list the images via the `images/index` template that we wrote and used in the `index/home` template:

```
                         4_displaying_images/templates/users/show.html

{{define "users/show"}}
<div class="row">
    <div class="col-md-12 col-xd-12">
        <div class="media">
            <a href="{{.User.ImagesRoute}}" class="pull-left">
                <img src="{{.User.AvatarURL}}" alt="{{.User.
➥Username}}">
            </a>
            <div class="media-body">
                <h1 class="media-heading">
                    {{.User.Username}}
```

```
                      {{if eq .User.ID  .CurrentUser.ID}}
                          <small>(this is you)</small>
                      {{end}}
                  </h1>
              </div>
          </div>
      </div>
</div>
{{template "images/index" .}}
{{end}}
```

There you have it. If you compile your code and browse around you'll now see a
working Gophr site where you can register, upload, and browse through photos.
Clicking on an avatar will take you to a page consisting solely of a user's images.
Go and take a look at your glorious masterpiece!

Summary

Congratulations on making it through to this point. We've covered a lot of different
areas in this chapter, so it's understandable if you're a feeling bit weary. We started
by looking at how Go provides a library for abstracting access to MySQL (or any
SQL database) through the `database/sql` package. We combined that with a Go
MySQL driver to power our image store. We also added functionality to upload
images from a user's computer and from a remote URL, which let us see how easy
it is to not only serve HTTP requests with Go, but to make them as well.

We're still not quite finished with Gophr. You may have noticed that we're serving
up the full image on every page, regardless of its size. In the next chapter, we'll look
at some of the powerful concurrency primitives available in Go and resize the images
to thumbnail and preview sizes once they're uploaded.

Exercises

You'll notice that there's no validation of the uploaded file in `CreateFromFile`. Add
in validation by checking that the extension of the uploaded file exists in the extension map used by `CreateFromURL`.

Gophr Part 5: Concurrency

In this chapter, we're going to look at resizing uploaded images to provide better performance and less wasted bandwidth on the Gophr site. To do this, we'll use a third-party image manipulation library. At the same time we're going to explore one of the most powerful aspects of Go that we're yet to cover: goroutines.

Goroutines

Goroutines are a way of running your code in an asynchronous manner, meaning that you can run more than one piece of code at the same time. Most web developers are familiar with this concept when talking about Ajax requests in the browser, where you make one or more requests from the page and deal with the response when it arrives via a callback; in the meantime you can continue running other code without requests blocking that code.

When it comes to the back end, however, most code is written in a synchronous manner, waiting for one block of code to complete before moving on to the next. While we may be processing several requests at the same time, each request is an inherently synchronous paradigm since it is independent of other requests and runs to completion quickly. Asynchronous code is different because it doesn't promise in a known time frame. If you make two asynchronous calls, they might finish in a different order every time you run the code. For example, making an Ajax request in JavaScript might provide a callback function to run:

```
get("http://example.com/api/results.json", function(results){
    console.log("Your results", results);
})
console.log("Requesting results");
```

You would expect the log to show `Requesting results` before displaying a line with `Your results`, because the `get` function is running code in an asynchronous manner. It won't block the main code from running, instead calling the callback when it's completed the call to `example.com`.

In Go, so far we've only written synchronous "blocking" code, where the code execution only continues once a piece of logic is finished. If I call a function, I expect it to run until it returns a value, then the rest of my code continues to execute. Here's some code that prints out the numbers one to ten:

```
package main

import "fmt"

func main(){
    count()
    fmt.Printf("Done")
}

func count(){
    for i := 1; i <= 10; i++ {
        fmt.Printf("%d,", i)
    }
}
```

If you run this code, you'll see `1,2,3,4,5,6,7,8,9,10,Done` outputted to your console. That's because when we call `count`, we're blocking the processing of our code. To run this code asynchronously inside a goroutine, we simply use the `go` command in front of the function call:

```
package main

import "fmt"

func main(){
    go count()
    fmt.Printf("Done")
}

func count(){
    for i := 1; i <= 10; i++ {
        fmt.Printf("%d,", i)
    }
}
```

If you run this code, all you will see this time is Done output to the console. That's because the count function no longer blocks the main function from executing. Because the main function continues executing, it prints Done and then finishes the program. Nothing in the count function has had a chance to run, or has told the main function to wait or block, so there's never the opportunity to start the loop.

If we alter our main function to wait for a while after we call the goroutine, we'll see the output return the count again. Here's the same example with a one-second wait after calling the count function:

```
package main

import (
    "fmt"
    "time"
)

func main() {
    go count()
    time.Sleep(time.Second)
    fmt.Printf("Done")
}

func count() {
    for i := 1; i <= 10; i++ {
```

```
        fmt.Printf("%d,", i)
    }
}
```

Running this code will see 1,2,3,4,5,6,7,8,9,10, printed to the console followed by a one-second wait, then Done will print too. No communication has happened between the count function and the main function; we've simply told it to wait for a second. This is terribly inefficient, since the count function was done well before that second was up. It's why we need methods for communication between goroutines and the code that calls them.

At this point, you're probably wondering why all the fuss? Admittedly, this example falls short of showing how this could be useful, but we need to understand the basic concepts first. Goroutines exist as a lightweight mechanism to create concurrent code that takes full advantage of the processing power available. A single CPU core can only run one piece of code at a time, but quite often your code isn't actually "running" per se, but waiting on external resources such as network calls or disk access. This sort of I/O blocks access to the CPU in most languages.

It's well known that most of the time in a web application request is spent accessing the database, and by freeing up the CPU for other code during these times, you can significantly increase the efficiency of your application. This alone makes Go a powerful tool, as although it may not make any one piece of code run faster, it allows more code to run, which in turn can translate to processing more requests on any individual piece of hardware. In fact, every request processed by the http package is run inside its own goroutine.

The other point to note, and this is important, is that goroutines allow you to easily scale your code across all the CPU cores that are available. Most modern systems have at least two, if not four, cores in their CPUs (along with possibly more than one CPU), and a single request to your website may only need to be handled by one of them. Later, we'll be using goroutines to resize images to multiple different resolutions at the same time by spreading the load across all the CPU cores on your system. This will significantly decrease the time taken to resize an image.

Waiting for Goroutines to Finish

Adding the `time.Sleep(time.Second)` call in the previous sectionwas a stopgap measure to show the code in action. In the real world you must communicate between goroutines and Go provides several ways to do this. If you don't have to deal with the result of a goroutine you can use `sync.WaitGroup`, which provides a simple interface while waiting for processes to complete. A wait group lets you add to a count with `Add(int)` in your main code and subtract from a count with `Done()` in your goroutines. You can then call `Wait()` in your main code and it will block the code until the goroutines have all called `Done`. Let's look at a slightly different example to see how a `WaitGroup` works:

```go
package main

import (
    "fmt"
    "sync"
    "time"
)

func main() {
    wg := sync.WaitGroup{}

    for i := 1; i <= 10; i++ {
        wg.Add(1)
        go func(j int) {
            time.Sleep(time.Duration(j) * time.Second)
            fmt.Printf("%d,", j)
            wg.Done()
        }(i)
    }

    fmt.Printf("Waiting:")
    wg.Wait()
    fmt.Printf("Done")
}
```

If you run this code, you'll see `Waiting:` output immediately, followed by a count every second until we hit 10 and `Done` will be output. A point of note is that we're using an anonymous function or **closure** here. That's a function that isn't named or assigned to a variable, but simply created and called immediately. We loop through one to ten, each time adding one to a wait group, then starting a goroutine that waits for j seconds before printing j and telling the wait group that it's done. Outside the `for` loop, you'll see we call `wg.Wait` to block the main code until such time as the wait group is considered done.

 Variable Scope

Within the code, you'll notice that the anonymous function takes a parameter `j int`, which we pass in as `i` from the loop. We do this because `j` is a copy of `i` when it comes into the anonymous function. If we tried to use the variable `i` (as we do the wait group `wg`), we'd find that by the time the goroutines actually start to process, the loop has finished and in every instance `i` would actually be equal to 11. This is because the variable `i` is created only once, then altered with each loop (`i` increments with each loop and when it increments to 11, it no longer satisfies the constraint `i <= 10` and the loop would complete). We can use the wait group directly inside the goroutine because wait groups are designed for concurrent access.

Communicating with Goroutines

If you need to know the results of your goroutines, then you need a way to communicate between them. Sharing access to memory between concurrently running code can often be a nightmare of locking and unlocking access to prevent race conditions from occurring when variables change unexpectedly. Go maintains a philosophy of "Don't communicate by sharing memory, share memory by communicating." Instead of having variables that are accessed by multiple goroutines, Go provides a method to communicate between goroutines so that you only have to access variables in a single coordinating scope.

To enable this communication, Go has a special primitive called the `channel`. **Channels** are a way to send and receive data between goroutines, and provide a way to block your code until you receive information on it. In reality, channels take a bit of mind power to comprehend, but once you understand them you'll see how they can be a clean and powerful way to communicate between multiple parts of your code.

Channels are typed and created with the `make` command. Here's an example creating a channel of type `int`:

```
myChan := make(chan int)
```

Sending and receiving on a channel happens with the <- command. By placing the arrow in front of the channel, you're saying that you want to receive from the channel (for example, myInt := <-myChan), whereas placing the arrow after the channel is how to send on a channel (for example, myChan <- 1). It's important to note that this is a blocking action. If you're sending on a channel and no code is ready to receive it, the execution will block, and vice versa when receiving on the channel, it will block if nothing is ready to send.

Channels can also be closed. By closing a channel, you're signifying that no more values will be sent over it and your code can continue. This enables us to range over a channel inside a loop, and have it break out of the loop once the channel is closed.

 Closing Channels

> It's unnecessary to close every channel you create. Closing a channel signifies that no more values will be sent on it; some code may wish to know that, while other code might not care. Go will automatically free up channels that are no longer sending or receiving from memory, so there is no performance hit to not closing a channel either.

Let's put this all together with an example based on our earlier counting code. We can use a channel to pass our numbers back to the main code to print:

```
package main

import (
    "fmt"
    "time"
)

func main() {
    intChan := make(chan int)
    for i := 1; i <= 10; i++ {
        go func(j int) {
            time.Sleep(time.Duration(j) * time.Second)
            intChan <- j
            if j == 10 {
```

```
                    close(intChan)
            }
        }(i)
    }

    for j := range intChan {
        fmt.Printf("%d,", j)
    }
    fmt.Println("Done")
}
```

So we create a new channel to pass back `int` values on, then loop through from one to ten. Inside each loop we run a function inside a goroutine that sleeps for j seconds, then sends back j on the channel. If the value of j is 10, we close the channel so that we can `range` over it. If the channel isn't closed, you'll see an error message: `fatal error: all goroutines are asleep - deadlock!`. Go has realized that the loop will never be closed and has freaked out. When developing Go applications you'll probably see this a fair bit, and that's okay. I prefer Go alerting us to this than having code that never completes and us being unable to figure out why.

After the loop, we range over the channel and print out the integer we receive on it. Keep in mind that while we range over the channel there are ten goroutines running at the same time, sleeping from one to ten seconds before sending back their delay integer. Only as those goroutines finish their sleep and send their integer back on the channel will the loop receive a value and run its code.

If you run this code now, you'll see what we did in the previous example: a count from one to ten with a second's delay between each count. The difference this time is that we're communicating between the goroutine and the main code, rather than printing directly from the goroutine.

Communicating with Multiple Channels

Go provides a simple method for waiting on messages from multiple channels and performing unique actions for each channel. You can wait for several channels to receive messages, and run different snippets of code whenever a channel receives a message. To do this, you use a `select` statement with a `case` for each channel. You may have seen `select` statements in programming languages before, where they are used as a streamlined `if`, `else if` statement, but this is slightly different:

```go
package main

import (
    "fmt"
    "math/rand"
    "time"
)

func wait(c chan int) {
    rand.Seed(time.Now().UnixNano())
    i := rand.Intn(5)
    time.Sleep(time.Duration(i) * time.Second)
    c <- i
}

func main() {
    chan1 := make(chan int)
    chan2 := make(chan int)
    go wait(chan1)
    go wait(chan2)

    select {
    case i := <-chan1:
        fmt.Printf("Received %d on chan 1", i)
    case i := <-chan2:
        fmt.Printf("Received %d on chan 2", i)
    }
}
```

In this example we have a function that takes a channel, generates a random integer from zero to five, waits for that many seconds, and then sends the integer on the supplied channel. We call this function inside a goroutine twice with a different channel each time. We then have a single `select` statement that waits for a result on either one of the channels. When the fastest call to `wait` completes, the `select` will run its code for the appropriate channel, then the code will continue on and the function completes. The second channel isn't received on, as the `select` statement can only receive on one channel at a time.

Using Channels and Selects for Timeouts

A `select` statement with two `channels` is a great way to handle timeouts in your code. If a goroutine is taking too long to process, you can choose to run other code instead. For example, if you needed to connect to an external service, you might want to return an error message if that service takes too long to respond. Let's have a look at creating a timeout when trying to retrieve the response from a Google search:

```go
package main

import (
    "fmt"
    "io/ioutil"
    "net/http"
    "time"
)

func main() {
    responseChan := make(chan *http.Response)
    go getURL(responseChan)

    timer := time.NewTimer(700 * time.Millisecond)

    select {
    case response := <-responseChan:
        body, _ := ioutil.ReadAll(response.Body)
        response.Body.Close()
        fmt.Printf("Received response: %s", string(body))

    case <-timer.C:
        fmt.Printf("Request timed out")
    }
}

func getURL(c chan *http.Response) {
    response, err := http.Get("https://www.google.co.nz/
➥search?q=golang")
    if err != nil {
        panic(err)
    }
    c <- response
}
```

This time we have a function that takes an `http.Response` channel and sends back the response from a Google query for `golang`. Note that you can have a channel that communicates almost any type, so a channel that passes a pointer to an `http.Re-`

sponse works perfectly. We run the function that calls Google in a goroutine and then create a `time.Timer` with the `time.NewTimer(time.Duration)` function. A `timer` struct has only one exported field, `C`, which is a channel that receives the current time after the duration supplied to `NewTimer` has passed. I found that about half my requests were responded to in under 700 milliseconds, so I've used that value here, but depending on your internet connection and location, you may need to adjust that value.

After this we have a `select` statement with a `case` for both the `responseChan` channel, which will get the response from Google, and the `time.Timer` channel, which will receive after 700 milliseconds. If you run this code, depending on how long Google takes to respond you might see the results of the request, or a timeout message if the request takes too long.

Looping on `selects`

On its own, a `select` statement with multiple channel `cases` will only receive on a single channel, so they are commonly combined with a `for` loop that repeats until you tell it to stop. A common example of this is when you have to poll for data at an interval, but also need a way to stop polling and continue on to the end of the function. In this example, we'll perform some action every second but stop if a stop channel is received on:

```
package main

import (
    "fmt"
    "time"
)

func main() {
    stopChan := make(chan bool)
    go func() {
        time.Sleep(4100 * time.Millisecond)
        stopChan <- true
    }()

    timer := time.NewTimer(time.Second)

    LOOP:
    for {
```

```
    select {
    case <-timer.C:
        // In reality you'd have some polling code here
        fmt.Println("Tick")
        timer.Reset(time.Second)
    case <-stopChan:
        fmt.Println("Boom")
        break LOOP
    }
  }
}
```

Instead of some other part of our code sending on the stopChan, we've just told it to do so some time after four seconds has passed—but that's just for this example. If you run this code you should see tick printed four times, followed by boom. Note that we've had to use what's called a named loop here, called LOOP (you can call it anything you like, though). The reason for this is that when we break out of the loop inside the select statement, Go will think we're trying to break out of the select statement rather than the for statement. By naming the loop and supplying that name to the break call, we're able to break out of both constructs with a single statement.

Throwing Away Goroutines

One last point on goroutines and channels is that you can happily ignore a channel if you'd prefer. Go is smart enough to know when there's no chance a value that's being sent on a channel will actually be received, so it won't hang on to those values in memory forever. You might wonder what sort of code would deliberately choose to ignore the results of a channel, so I'll refer to an example that the Go creators themselves use.

Pretend that you're Google, and your entire business is built on being the fastest search engine around. To reach this level of performance, you could have multiple back ends that you query for every search and just return results from the first one to respond, throwing away the other results. This method of over-provisioning your infrastructure is a trade-off between cost and performance. It costs more to run the extra capacity of those back ends since your searches are being run more times than they need to, but the result is that your average response times are lower:

```
package main

var backends := []string{
    "http://example.org/backend1",
    "http://example.org/backend2",
    "http://example.org/backend3",
}

func main() {
    query := "some search query"
    results := make(chan SearchResults)
    for _, backend := range backends {
        // Send the request to the backend
        go queryBackend(query, backend, results)
    }

    result := <-results:
    handleResult(result)
}
```

Here you can see some example code that takes a search query and sends it to each back end in an array via the imaginary queryBackend function. We then select the channel we've sent, which would theoretically be sent three results, but since we only have a single select we're only ever going to read one result off the channel. The others will just be ignored, and we'll only deal with the first—or fastest—result. We've also added a timeout for good measure.

Putting Goroutines into Practice

Now it's time to actually put goroutines into practice in the Gophr app. When we're uploading our images, we're doing no resizing at all. This means that every time a user downloads a thumbnail of the image on the index page, or even the image on the show page itself, they're downloading much more than necessary. Since we show the image in two sizes, we need to resize the image so that it's appropriate for each display type: a square thumbnail on the index/user pages, and a larger image on the main page. By keeping the thumbnail square, we'll allow the list pages to align easily while keeping the correct image proportions when viewing it in detail.

To do the image resizing, we're going to use the library called Imaging[1] by Grigory Dryapak. This is an image resizing and altering library written in pure Go that provides a simple interface to a variety of image manipulation tasks. While we'll only use the image resizing features, the library is also capable of image manipulation such as contrast adjustment, blur, and sharpening.

imaging Version

The version of imaging that I'm using is Git commit 4685da8.[2] If you have trouble with the current version of imaging, you can ensure compatibility with the examples in this book by checking out this commit. See the notes at the start of the book for instructions on how to do this.

Multiple Methods

Since we're creating different aspect ratio images, it's easier to create two methods than a single method to which we pass different parameters. We're also going to create approximate resizes. Bootstrap gives us a responsive design by default so it's hard to create pixel-perfect resized images; it also wouldn't consider Retina displays that can display even more pixels. This sort of content is outside the scope of this book, but you can rest assured that if you were to need other sizes, you'd be able to quickly create them too.

We'll be adding a method called CreateResizedImages to our Image type that resizes and saves the image to disk in the two sizes we want. This in turn will call two methods, one for each resize: resizeThumbnail and resizePreview:

```
                                      1_image_resizing/image.go (excerpt)
import  (
    ⋮
    "runtime"
    ⋮
    "github.com/disintegration/imaging"
)

func init() {
```

---

[1] https://github.com/disintegration/imaging/
[2] https://github.com/disintegration/imaging/tree/4685da8f7d9ed48a7d6b8982fd966d4fd83b4d2e

```
        // Ensure our goroutines run across all cores
        runtime.GOMAXPROCS(runtime.NumCPU())
}

    ⋮

func (image *Image) CreateResizedImages() error {
        // Generate an image from file
        srcImage, err := imaging.Open("./data/images/" + image.Location)
        if err != nil {
            return err
        }

        // Create a channel to receive errors on
        errorChan := make(chan error)

        // Process each size
        go image.resizePreview(errorChan, srcImage)
        go image.resizeThumbnail(errorChan, srcImage)

        // Wait for images to finish resizing
        var err error
        for i := 0; i < 2; i++ {
            err := <-errorChan
            if err == nil {
                err = e
            }
        }
        return err
}
```

The first item of note is that we've made a call to `runtime.GOMAXPROCS` with the result of `runtime.NumCPU`. This is basically telling Go that it can process on as many CPUs as the computer has. By default Go will only process on a single CPU, which is unhelpful when we're trying to spread the load across more than one.

Then you'll see that we've created our new method `CreateResizedImages`. This method starts by opening the source image file using the `imaging` library. We then create a channel used to return any errors that occur while processing the image in a goroutine. We start two goroutines, one each for the two resizing methods; then we receive from the channel twice in a loop, each time assigning the error to our previously declared error variable if it's yet to be set. We use this simple `for` loop because we know in our code that we've only created two goroutines, so we'll only ever obtain two results on the channel. If we weren't to run the two methods in goroutines, they'd run sequentially on a single CPU core; they'll actually run across two cores if your system has them, allowing them to be processed much faster.

Handling All Errors

We could have returned early if we discovered an error; however, it would mean that if we received an error on the first iteration of the loop and returned, the second iteration would never occur and the second goroutine never complete. This would cause the goroutine to remain in memory.

Let's take a look at the method `resizeThumbnail` first. This is the method that resizes the source image into a square image; we'll make the width and height 400 pixels. This is more than enough for the thumbnails we'll display, but still significantly smaller than the source image is likely to be:

```
                                          1_image_resizing/image.go (excerpt)

var widthThumbnail = 400

func (image *Image) resizeThumbnail(errorChan chan error, srcImage
➥image.Image) {
    dstImage := imaging.Thumbnail(srcImage, widthThumbnail,
➥widthThumbnail, imaging.Lanczos)

    destination := "./data/images/thumbnail/" + image.Location
    errorChan <- imaging.Save(dstImage, destination)
}
```

As you can see, the method takes the channel on which we send back any errors, and the `image.Image` instance that we created by opening the source file with the `imaging` library. The `imaging` library has a very simple `Thumbnail` function that takes an image, width, and height, and a resampling algorithm. Once we have a new resampled image, we send on the channel the result of saving the file to a new subdirectory `thumbnail` within the `data/images` folder.

Image Resampling Algorithms

You can use one of several resampling algorithms with the `imaging` library. Lanczos resampling is generally considered to be a good choice as a general-purpose resampling algorithm. The algorithms themselves are beyond the scope of this book, but feel free to look into the alternatives provided in the `imaging` package source code. For more information, you can check out the Wikipedia article on Image Scaling.[3]

The `resizePreview` method is a little more complicated. We'll be resizing our preview images to 800 pixels wide but, unlike the thumbnail resize, we'll be sticking to the original image's aspect ratio. This means that we'll need to work out the new height based on the original aspect ratio with a width of 800:

```
                                          1_image_resizing/image.go (excerpt)
var widthPreview = 800

func (image *Image) resizePreview(errorChan chan error, srcImage
➥image.Image) {
    size := srcImage.Bounds().Size()
    ratio := float64(size.Y) / float64(size.X)
    targetHeight := int(float64(widthPreview) * ratio)

    dstImage := imaging.Resize(srcImage, widthPreview, targetHeight,
➥imaging.Lanczos)

    destination := "./data/images/preview/" + image.Location
    errorChan <- imaging.Save(dstImage, destination)
}
```

To figure out the target height of the image, we work out the aspect ratio. We can obtain the size information from the source image, which returns a struct with the X and Y sizes. We need to convert them to `float64` from `int` to ensure that the resulting ratio isn't rounded to a whole number. Once we have the ratio, we can multiply it by the `widthPreview` (which is 800), and then convert back into an `int`. This gives us integers for both `widthPreview` and `targetHeight`, which we send into the `imaging.Resize` function, then save into the subdirectory `preview` in `data/images`.

All that's left now for the resizing is to actually call the `CreateResizedImages` method when uploading the images. To do this, we call the method and check for errors just before we return from the methods `CreateFromFile` and `CreateFromURL`:

---

[3] http://en.wikipedia.org/wiki/Image_scaling

```go
func (image *Image) CreateFromURL(imageURL string) error {

    ⋮

    // Create the various resizes of the images
    err = image.CreateResizedImages()
    if err != nil {
        return err
    }

    // Save our image to the store
    return globalImageStore.Save(image)
}

func (image *Image) CreateFromFile(file multipart.File, headers
➥*multipart.FileHeader) error {

    ⋮

    // Create the various resizes of the images
    err = image.CreateResizedImages()
    if err != nil {
        return err
    }

    // Save our image to the store
    return globalImageStore.Save(image)
}
```

You must create the thumbnail and preview directory in data/images before running this code, otherwise Go will be unable to write correctly. Once you've created those directories, you can compile and run the Gophr server. If youupload an image see that we're getting resized images in the thumbnail and preview directories, as shown in Figure 8.1. One of the interesting aspects to note here is that the CreateResizedImages method is a synchronous interface that contains an asynchronous implementation. The calling code is completely unaware of the concurrent implementation under the hood. We could swap the implementation with a synchronous one without having to update how it was called.

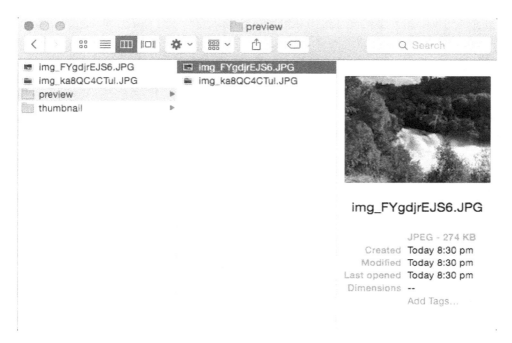

Figure 8.1. The resized images will have the same filename but be within their subdirectories

Using the Resized Images

Our last task is to set up our templates to look for the resized images. To do this we'll add two more route methods on the `Image` type—one that returns the path for the thumbnail image, and one for the preview image:

```
2_display_resized/image.go (excerpt)

func (image *Image) StaticThumbnailRoute() string {
    return "/im/thumbnail/" + image.Location
}
func (image *Image) StaticPreviewRoute() string {
    return "/im/preview/" + image.Location
}
```

These are self-explanatory and very similar to the `StaticRoute` method that we're using currently, except we've included the subdirectories as well so the correct resized image will be served up.

Lastly, we'll find in our template where we've been referencing the `StaticRoute` method and replace it with the appropriate resized image. Since we used a partial template for listing the images in both the home page and the user page, we only have to replace two occurrences—one for each size. Replace the reference to `StaticRoute` in `templates/images/index.html` to `StaticThumbnailRoute`, and `templates/images/show.html` to `StaticPreviewRoute`.

Once you've replaced those references, compile your code and you're done! You now have a complete Gophr site that resizes and displays uploaded images. Well done.

Summary

That's it for our Gophr example application. I hope you've seen how easy it can be to create a web application from the ground up in Go with mostly just the standard library. We've seen how interfaces have enabled creating swappable storage back ends for sessions, users, and images, and we've seen how Go can run code in goroutines to harness the full power and speed of modern hardware.

In the next chapters, we're going look at automated testing of your code, how to manage deploying your code to production servers, and some tips on managing your code as it grows.

9

Automated Testing

For a long time in the web development world, automated testing was unlikely to be part of a developers' toolkit. Nowadays, a test suite is an integral part of most successful projects, libraries, and frameworks. An **automated test suite** is a series of tests that can be run to ensure that the business logic of your code is behaving as it should. There are a variety of test types: from checking the end-to-end processes of your code, to simply testing that a single function or method does as it's supposed to. In this chapter, we'll look at the tools that Go provides out of the box for writing and running a test suite.

Writing tests at the start of a project is a great way to explore the requirements of a set piece of work, as you must be able to describe exactly how the pieces will fit together, what inputs they'll take, and what outputs they'll provide. Even if you don't write your tests at the start, a test suite that takes account of the inputs and expected outputs of your systems means that you can change your code with a level of confidence: if the code no longer work as expected, the tests will break and you'll be alerted to the issue. For example, if you've written tests that check a user logging in, you can rest assured that if the tests are passing the process is functioning, even if you've changed the way the underlying code works.

Writing Tests in Go

Writing tests in Go is fairly straightforward. The code is written in Go, and you run it through the tool `go test`. To produce a test suite, create a file with a name that ends in `_test.go`. Any test function in this file will be executed by the `go test` tool. A test function is a function with the name `TestXxx`, where `Xxxx` is any other alphanumeric string not starting with a lowercase letter. It takes a single parameter that is an instance of `*testing.T`. An example test function might look like this:

```
func TestNewUser(t *testing.T) {
  // Test some functionality in here
}
```

Go will not normally include any code you write in a test file; that is, any file ending in **_test.go**. As a result, you can write almost any Go code you'd like in these files. You can define new functions, data types, interfaces, and so on—it's all just Go code. We'll have a look at how this benefits us later on, but for now, let's take a look at how we actually test some code.

Passing and Failing

Tests are generally marked as either passing or failing. A successful test run must have all tests passing, and is often referred to as being "green," since many test systems mark passes in green. As you might expect, a failing test suite is "red," for obvious reasons.

The `*testing.T` parameter that each Go test receives as a parameter has a `Fail` method that you can call to fail a test, and an `Error` method that you can use to fail a test along with a message. If you don't actively fail a test, it's presumed to be passing. For example, you might have two tests, `TestOnePlusOneIsTwo` and `TestTwoPlusTwoIsFour`:

```
                                          examples/1_addition/addition_test.go
package main

import "testing"

func TestOnePlusOne(t *testing.T) {
    onePlusOne := 1 + 1
```

```
    if onePlusOne != 2 {
        t.Error("Expected 1 + 1 to equal 2, but got", onePlusOne)
    }
}

func TestTwoPlusTwo(t *testing.T) {
    twoPlusTwo := 2 + 2
    if twoPlusTwo != 5 {
        t.Error("Expected 2 + 2 to equal 5, but got", twoPlusTwo)
    }
}
```

If you place this code in a file `addition_test.go` and then run `go test` inside the
same directory, you'll see output like this:

```
--- FAIL: TestTwoPlusTwo (0.00 seconds)
    addition_test.go:16: Expected 2 + 2 to equal 5, but got 4
FAIL
exit status 1
FAIL    ./chapter9/examples/1_addition 0.007s
```

We see no mention of the passing test `TestOnePlusOne`, which is how we want
it—we only really care about failing tests. We see that there's a failure in test
`TestTwoPlusTwo`, as well as the output message that we wrote in our code. If we fix
up the expectation from 5 to 4 (as it obviously should be) and rerun the tests, we
see a different message:

```
PASS
ok      ./chapter9/examples/1_addition    0.007s
```

This time no test fails, so we see a pass message output to the terminal. This is great,
since it indicates that all the tests have run and every time we've expected a value
to equal another value, it's been correct. These expectations form the building blocks
of what can often be very complex test situations that cover all the various aspects
of our systems.

Testing Multiple Variations of Inputs

Clearly the previous counting example was contrived to show the way we pass or fail tests. A more useful example will utilize some of the code we wrote in the Gophr project from previous chapters.

One of the more important parts of the Gophr project was the `NewUser` function, which was responsible for taking a username, password, and email address, and checking if they were valid inputs from which to create a new user. A variety of validations are performed, such as checking the password length, or whether a user already exists with the supplied username or email address. All the different combinations of inputs to validate are perfect candidates for automated tests.

To test the more basic input validations, such as the existence of a username and email, we can simply pass in invalid strings and test the returned value. As a reminder, the signature of the `NewUser` function is `func NewUser(username, email, password string) (User, error)`:

```
                                              1_simple_input_tests/user_test.go

package main

import "testing"

func TestNewUserNoUsername(t *testing.T) {
    _, err := NewUser("", "user@example.com", "password")
    if err != errNoUsername {
        t.Error("Expected err to be errNoUsername")
    }
}

func TestNewUserNoPassword(t *testing.T) {
    _, err := NewUser("user", "user@example.com", "")
    if err != errNoPassword {
        t.Error("Expected err to be errNoUsername")
    }
}
```

In `TestNewUserNoUsername`, we check that the error returned is `errNoUsername` when we attempt to create a user with no username; in `TestNewUserNoPassword`, we do the same with `errNoPassword`. These tests prove that the validation we have for empty usernames and passwords is still working. If we rewrite `NewUser` and the tests still pass, we're safe to assume nothing has broken.

We can continue to test the presence of an email address and the length of the password, but as these are very similar to the previous example, I'll leave it up to you to test them in your own time. Instead, we'll look at the next part of the `NewUser` function, where we attempt to retrieve a user from the `globalUserStore`. To test the reaction when we try to create a user whose username or email already exists, we could write code that enters those users into the database and then deletes them afterwards, but that would be a bit complicated. Instead, we can safely create mock responses by assigning our own instance of `UserStore` into the `globalUserStore` variable. This is when all the work we did in defining interfaces will start to pay off.

The term **mock** in testing refers to creating a fake version of a type that we use to control the parameters of a test. If we create a mock `UserStore` and tell it to return a user when `FindByUsername` is called, we test that the behavior seen when the `NewUser` function is run is correct.

To create a mock `UserStore` instance, we define a new type and the appropriate methods to implement `UserStore`. Because this type will only be compiled when we run the test suite, it won't pollute the application when we compile it normally. To make it versatile, we'll assign fields for each of the `Find` methods to return, and a field for the `Save` method to assign the user it receives to. This allows us to fake the response to a specific method call, and test the behavior:

2_mock_interface/user_test.go (excerpt)

```
type MockUserStore struct {
    findUser        *User
    findEmailUser   *User
    findUsernameUser *User
    saveUser        *User
}

func (store *MockUserStore) Find(string) (*User, error) {
    return store.findUser, nil
}

func (store *MockUserStore) FindByEmail(string) (*User, error) {
    return store.findEmailUser, nil
```

```
}

func (store *MockUserStore) FindByUsername(string) (*User, error) {
    return store.findUsernameUser, nil
}

func (store *MockUserStore) Save(user *User) error {
    store.saveUser = user
    return nil
}
```

Each of the `Find` methods, which return a pointer to a user or an error, simply return the appropriate user from the `MockUserStore` and no error. In our tests, we can now create a new `MockUserStore` and test the effects when `FindByUsername` and `FindByEmail` return users:

```
                                    2_mock_interface/user_test.go (excerpt)

func TestNewUserExistingUsername(t *testing.T) {
    globalUserStore = &MockUserStore{
        findUsernameUser: &User{},
    }

    _, err := NewUser("user", "user@example.com", "somepassword")
    if err != errUsernameExists {
        t.Error("Expected err to be errUsernameExists")
    }
}

func TestNewUserExistingEmail(t *testing.T) {
    globalUserStore = &MockUserStore{
        findEmailUser: &User{},
    }

    _, err := NewUser("user", "user@example.com", "somepassword")
    if err != errEmailExists {
        t.Error("Expected err to be errEmailExists")
    }
}
```

With the `TestNewUserExistingUsername` and `TestNewUserExistingEmail` tests, we assign a `MockUserStore` instance to the `globalUserStore` var, which the `NewUser` function calls. This mock instancereturns a user for the `FindByUsername` or `Find-`

ByEmail in the appropriate test, and we expect to see a corresponding error returned when we attempt to call NewUser with valid inputs. We can now be sure that we'll avoid having users with duplicate usernames or emails as long as this test continues to pass.

Code Coverage

Go also provides tools to generate **code coverage** reports. These reports will tell us exactly how much of your code has been tested. While sometimes it might make little sense to target 100% code coverage, (checking the result of every single if err != nil block can be tedious and take more time than it's worth), it's definitely a great way to check for any areas in your code that you might not be testing.

To run a code coverage test, you will first need to install the cover tool by running go get code.google.com/p/go.tools/cmd/cover. Once this tool is installed, you can run go test with the flag -coverprofile cover.out, and Go will create a file **cover.out** with a coverage report, printing coverage information to the terminal. Running this for our current tests produces an 8.9% coverage report:

```
PASS
coverage: 8.9% of statements
ok  ./chapter9/2_mock_interface 0.015s
```

The cover tool also provides a way to generate a visual HTML page of coverage information for each file. You can run this with go tool cover -html=cover.out. When you run it, you'll see a web page pop up in your default browser with a drop-down menu itemfor each file in the project, and the code highlighted in a combination of gray, red, and green, as seen in Figure 9.1.

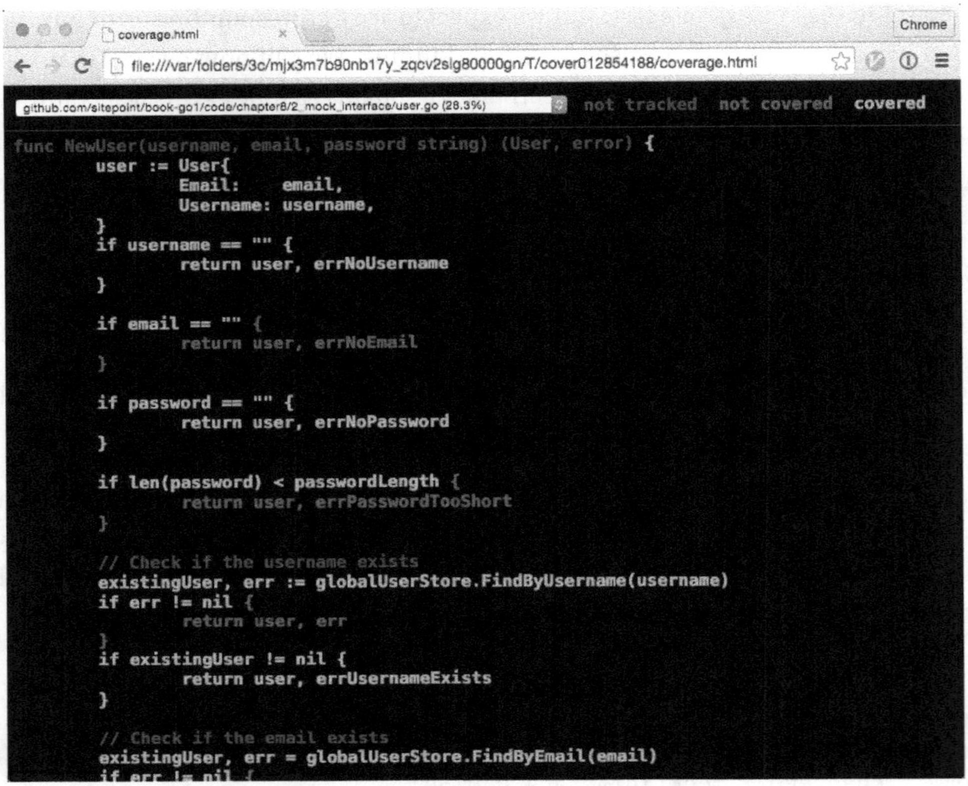

Figure 9.1. Our NewUser function's coverage report

The **user.go** test report shows that our coverage of NewUser is fairly good so far. We've checked that the username and password exist, but we're not checking whether the email exists or the password length is appropriate. We can also see that we're checking whether a user exists with the same username, but we're not testing to see what happens if the FindByUsername method returns an error.

Testing Between Packages

Interfaces are an ideal way to mock out parts of your code while testing; however, they're not always the best solution for mocking parts of your code. If the only reason an interface exists is to allow you to create a mock interface in your tests, chances are it's introducing more complexity in your codebase than is required. Interfaces are also unable to solve the problem when packages out of your control return different responses to testing. How would we test what happens when we're unable to save the FileUserStore to disk?

A method that I use extensively in these cases is to assign the function I want to call to a variable, and then call the variable as if it were the function. Once assigned to a variable, the function can be replaced with another function during tests. Let's look at a simplified example of this, where we write out a string to a file and need to test the outcome:

examples/2_wrapper_functions/main.go *(excerpt)*

```go
package main

import (
    "io/ioutil"
    "os"
)

func main() {
    str := "How do I test this message is being written?"
    loc := "test.txt"
    err := WriteStuff(str, loc)
    if err != nil {
        panic(err)
    }
}

func WriteStuff(str, loc string) error {
    return ioutil.WriteFile(loc, []byte(str), os.ModeAppend)
}
```

The function WriteStuff takes two parameters: the string to write and the location to write to. It then uses the ioutil.WriteFile method to do the actual writing of the file. If we simply wanted to test that the correct values are being passed to the WriteFile function, or even just prevent the call from actually writing to file in our tests, we need to be able to control the ioutil.WriteFile function, which we can't. Instead, we assign ioutil.WriteFile to a variable:

examples/2_wrapper_functions/main.go *(excerpt)*

```go
func WriteStuff(str, loc string) error {
    err := writeFile(loc, []byte(str), os.ModeAppend)
    if err != nil {
        return err
    }
    return nil
```

```
}

var writeFile = ioutil.WriteFile
```

We now have a function stored in the variable `writeFile`, which contains the function `ioutil.WriteFile`. If this was to be run now, nothing has changed except for calling our local variable instead. What's great about this is that when we run our tests, we can replace the function that's stored in `writeFile` with a completely different function. Only the function signature `func(loc string, data []byte, perm os.FileMode) error` needs to stay the same, since that is the type of the variable.

Now we can swap out the `writeFile` function, we can test that the values being passed into `WriteStuff` flow through to the call to `writeFile`:

```
                                    examples/2_wrapper_functions/main_test.go
package main

import (
    "os"
    "testing"
)

func TestWriteStuff(t *testing.T) {
    testStr := "Test String"
    testLoc := "testfile.txt"

    // Store the current writeFile and reinstate it at the end of
➥the test
    oldWriteFile := writeFile
    defer func() {
        writeFile = oldWriteFile
    }()

    // Create a new function that tests the passed parameters
    writeFile = func(loc string, data []byte, perm os.FileMode)
➥error {
        if loc != testLoc {
            t.Error("Expected loc to be", testLoc, "but got", loc)
        }
        if string(data) != testStr {
            t.Error("Expected data to be", testStr, "but got",
```

```
➡string(data))
        }
        return nil
    }

    err := WriteStuff(testStr, testLoc)
    if err != nil {
        t.Error("Expected no error, but got", err)
    }
}
```

Looking at this test function, we can see that we're creating a new variable oldWrite-File that contains the current value of writeFile. We do this so that once our test has run, we can put back the original function into writeFile. This is a matter of housekeeping, but it's very important since other tests will most likely end up calling the function and expect its normal behavior. To replace the value when we're finished, we create an anonymous function that assigns the old value back and run it with the defer command. This defer will ensure that the variable is replaced whenever the test function finishes running, and keeps the logic of replacing the writeFile grouped in the same place.

Once we've ensured that we can replace writeFile at the end of the function, we can go ahead and clobber it with a new function specifically for the test. The new writeFile function shares the same function signature and tests the values that are passed in to make sure they match the values expected.

The last part of the test calls the WriteStuff function and checks that no error is returned. Now we have a test that passes as long as the values are passed through and no error is returned.

We can now add a test function for the behavior where an error is thrown when trying to write the file. Any error returned from writeFile should be returned from WriteStuff:

```
func TestWriteStuffError(t *testing.T) {
    testStr := "Test String"
    testLoc := "testfile.txt"
    testErr := errors.New("Ah! An error.")

    // Store the current writeFile and reinstate it at the end of
```

```
➥the test
    oldWriteFile := writeFile
    defer func() {
        writeFile = oldWriteFile
    }()

    // create a new function that returns an error
    writeFile = func(loc string, data []byte, perm os.FileMode)
➥error {
        return testErr
    }

    err := WriteStuff(testStr, testLoc)
    if err != testErr {
        t.Error("Expected an error, but got", err)
    }
}
```

The `TestWriteStuffError` function is very similar to `TestWriteStuff`, except instead of testing the values that come into the `writeFile` function, we return a known error that we created, and check that the error returned when we call `WriteStuff` is the same error. If you run this test code now, you'll see that we receive two passes! Sometimes when tests pass it's nice to break expectations (for example, by changing a != to a ==), just to see them fail, to be sure. Then again, perhaps it's just me that likes to do that.

Testing HTTP Requests and Responses

The final element that I'd like to look at regarding testing in Go is how we test HTTP requests. If we're running a production service with authentication, we want to rest assured that the behavior we expect hasn't suddenly changed! Likewise, we want to be able to test what happens when our code makes its own HTTP requests, such as when the Gophr project from the previous chapters uploads a file from an external server.

Testing the Gophr Authentication

We'll continue adding tests to the `Gophr` project with a test that checks what happens when you ask for the "New Image" page—both when you're logged out, and logged in. To test the logged out behavior, we'll just request the page and check that we're redirected to the login page. Testing the logged in behavior is a bit more tricky: we'll need to create a `MockSessionInterface` that we can use along with a cookie.

To test requests to our application, we're after a way to record the response to a specific request. Luckily the Go standard library rides in on a gopher and comes to the rescue once again. A handy testing library called `httptest` provides all that we need to record the response from any application request. The one complication is that the entire application is currently set up in our `main` function, which won't run when using the test suite. To make setting up the application easier in the tests, we'll move the creation of routes into another function `NewApp`, which returns a fully loaded router ready to run:

3_http_testing/main.go (excerpt)

```go
func main(){
    log.Fatal(http.ListenAndServe(":3000", NewApp()))
}

func NewApp() Middleware {
    router := NewRouter()

    router.Handle("GET", "/", HandleHome)
    router.Handle("GET", "/register", HandleUserNew)
    router.Handle("POST", "/register", HandleUserCreate)
    router.Handle("GET", "/login", HandleSessionNew)
    router.Handle("POST", "/login", HandleSessionCreate)
    router.Handle("GET", "/image/:imageID", HandleImageShow)
    router.Handle("GET", "/user/:userID", HandleUserShow)

    router.ServeFiles(
        "/assets/*filepath",
        http.Dir("assets/"),
    )
    router.ServeFiles(
        "/im/*filepath",
        http.Dir("data/images/"),
    )

    secureRouter := NewRouter()
    secureRouter.Handle("GET", "/sign-out", HandleSessionDestroy)
    secureRouter.Handle("GET", "/account", HandleUserEdit)
    secureRouter.Handle("POST", "/account", HandleUserUpdate)
    secureRouter.Handle("GET", "/images/new", HandleImageNew)
```

```
        secureRouter.Handle("POST", "/images/new", HandleImageCreate)

        middleware := Middleware{}
        middleware.Add(router)
        middleware.Add(http.HandlerFunc(RequireLogin))
        middleware.Add(secureRouter)

        return middleware
}
```

All of the routing code here is the same as before; it's just nicely encapsulated in a single method that we call in `main` and can call in our tests too.

So how do we test the response? We need to create a `httptest.ResponseRecorder` and pass it as the `http.ResponseWriter` to our application's `ServerHTTP` function, along with a request for the appropriate path. This simulates our application actually receiving a request for the path, and we can then have some expectations against the response we get. When we redirect a user, we do so by returning a 301 HTTP status code and adding a `Location` header, which tells the browser where it should redirect to. These are the two pieces of information for which we'll be making expectations:

3_http_testing/auth_test.go *(excerpt)*

```
package main

import (
    "net/http"
    "testing"
)

func TestRequestNewImageUnauthenticated(t *testing.T) {
    request, _ := http.NewRequest("GET", "/images/new", nil)
    recorder := httptest.NewRecorder()

    app := NewApp()
    app.ServeHTTP(recorder, request)

    if recorder.Code != http.StatusFound {
        t.Error("Expected a redirect code, but got", recorder.Code)
    }
```

```
    loc := recorder.HeaderMap.Get("Location")
    if loc != "/login?next=%252Fimages%252Fnew" {
        t.Error("Expected Location to redirect to sign in, but got",
➥loc)
    }
}
```

To start with, we create a function `TestRequestNewImageUnauthenticated`. This function begins by creating a `http.Request` to the `/images/new` path, and a `httptest.ResponseRecorder` that we'll use to record the response. We create an instance of our application with `NewApp`, and then tell the application to respond to the request we created by writing to our recorder. Since `httptest.ResponseRecorder` implements the `http.ResponseWriter` interface, we can do this—and the recorder will record what the `ServeHTTP` method has written to it. Once we have the response, we're able to check that the response code stored in the field `Code` and the `Location` header are the values we're expecting. If you run this test right now, you will see it successfully passing.

The next step is to test what happens when a user is authenticated. To do this, we'll need to provide a session cookie in our request that matches a stored session. We can do this by creating a `MockSessionStore` type assigned to `globalSessionStore`, and return an appropriate session when it's called. We can keep the `MockSessionStore` simple for the moment, with just a field `Session` that we assign a value that `Find` should return. We don't need to deal with the `Save` and `Delete` methods that the `SessionStore` interface defines; we'll just create functions that return `nil`. We'll also make use of our `MockUserStore` from earlier in this chapter:

3_http_testing/auth_test.go (excerpt)

```
func TestRequestNewImageAuthenticated(t *testing.T) {
    // Replace the user store temporarily
    oldUserStore := globalUserStore
    defer func() {
        globalUserStore = oldUserStore
    }()
    globalUserStore = &MockUserStore{
        findUser: &User{},
    }

    expiry := time.Now().Add(time.Hour)
```

```go
    // Replace the session store temporarily
    oldSessionStore := globalSessionStore
    defer func() {
        globalSessionStore = oldSessionStore
    }()
    globalSessionStore = &MockSessionStore{
        Session: &Session{
            ID:     "session_123",
            UserID: "user_123",
            Expiry: expiry,
        },
    }

    // Create a cookie for the
    authCookie := &http.Cookie{
        Name:    sessionCookieName,
        Value:   "session_123",
        Expires: expiry,
    }

    request, _ := http.NewRequest("GET", "/images/new", nil)
    request.AddCookie(authCookie)

    recorder := httptest.NewRecorder()

    app := NewApp()
    app.ServeHTTP(recorder, request)

    if recorder.Code != http.StatusOK {
        t.Error("Expected a redirect code, but got", recorder.Code)
    }
}
```

The first task in our function is to assign new mock stores to globalUserStore and globalSessionStore. Then we create a new cookie token named as the session code expects. The session and the cookie expire in an hour since we need to have a future value on them, otherwise they'll be expired for us. We add the cookie to the request with AddCookie, then make the request as we did before. This time there's no need to check against the Location header; all we have to do is make sure that we receive a 200 response, represented by the constant http.StatusOK.

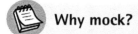 **Why mock?**

You might be thinking at this point "Why don't we just create the user and session in the standard file stores?" The answer to this lies in the speed and scope of the testing. We could definitely do this, but it translates that a lot more work is going on with the writing and reading of files. Computers are fast so it will happen very quickly, but as Gophr grows and you add more tests, this code will run hundreds or thousands of times and it will slow down the entire test suite. If tests have already been written that cover the functionality of the `FileUserStore` and `FileSessionStore`, there's no need to continue testing the functionality as part of other tests. A good approach when testing is to test small units of functionality in isolation, and test them well. Doing this rather than relying on testing the entire process from end to end will make bugs faster to track down, and your code more maintainable in the long run, although end-to-end tests have their place too.

Testing Remote HTTP requests

So far we've looked at testing the requests that we're making to the Gophr project, but how do we test the requests the Gophr project is making to external services? An example would be when we provide a URL to an image and Gophr attempts to download it.

The `httptest` library saves the day again with the `httptest.Server` type. This allows us to create a server with a handler function that we can quickly set up to respond to our image download requests. We'll test a couple of scenarios that we dealt with in the `CreateImageFromURL` method by returning different status codes and headers from the server's handler function:

```
                                      3_http_testing/image_test.go (excerpt)

package main

import (
    "net/http"
    "net/http/httptest"
    "testing"
)

func TestImageCreateFromURLInvalidStatusCode(t *testing.T) {
    server := httptest.NewServer(http.HandlerFunc(func(w http.
➥ResponseWriter, r *http.Request) {
```

```
                w.WriteHeader(404)
        }))
        defer server.Close()

        image := Image{}
        err := image.CreateFromURL(server.URL)
        if err != errImageURLInvalid {
            t.Errorf("Expected errImageURLInvalid but got %s", err)
        }
}

func TestImageCreateFromURLInvalidContentType(t *testing.T) {
        server := httptest.NewServer(http.HandlerFunc(func(w http.
➥ResponseWriter, r *http.Request) {
            w.WriteHeader(200)
            w.Header().Add("Content-Type", "text/html")
        }))
        defer server.Close()

        image := Image{}
        err := image.CreateFromURL(server.URL)
        if err != errInvalidImageType {
            t.Errorf("Expected errInvalidImageType but got %s", err)
        }
}
```

In our first test function, TestImageCreateFromURLInvalidStatusCode, we create a new server with a handler that returns a 404 status code and defer closing it until the end of the function. We then create a new Image and attempt to download it at the server's URL. We check that the response error is the correct type: errImageURLInvalid. In the next function TestImageCreateFromURLInvalidContentType we return a 200 OK response code, but this time return an invalid Content-Type header and check that we get a errInvalidImageType error. These two very small test functions have now tested the two invalid response types for which the CreateImageFromURL method checks.

Performance Benchmarking

The last topic we'll cover in this chapter is some basic performance benchmarking. Go provides a simple method for benchmarking code as part of the testing package. For instance, how any function starting with Test will run as a test function, or a function starting with `Benchmark` and taking an instance of `*testing.B` will run as a benchmark.

The `testing.B` type contains a single exported field `N`. This field is an integer that defines how many times a benchmark should be run. The idea is that you should run some code inside a loop that runs `N` times, and Go will adjust `N` as the benchmark progresses so that an appropriate number of iterations occur, but without the entire benchmarking taking too long.

For example, if we wanted to benchmark how long it takes to response to an unauthorised request, we can run the request like we did in our earlier test cases inside the benchmark loop:

```
                                            4_benchmarking/auth_test.go (excerpt)
func BenchmarkRequestNewImageUnauthenticated(b *testing.B) {
    request, _ := http.NewRequest("GET", "/images/new", nil)

    recorder := httptest.NewRecorder()
    app := NewApp()

    for i := 0; i < b.N; i++ {
        app.ServeHTTP(recorder, request)
    }
}
```

There's no need to create the app instance or request inside the loop—in fact, this would misrepresent the actual time taken to respond (although it takes an almost negligible amount of time to create the app). The only element we're testing in the loop is how long it takes for the app to respond to the request.

To run the tests with benchmarks, we'll run `go test -bench ..` The flag `-bench` lets Go know we want to run benchmarks. The period after the `-bench` flag is important; you can also add a regular expression there to run only benchmarks that match, but the period means that it should run all benchmarks:

```
PASS
BenchmarkRequestNewImageUnauthenticated    500000             4837 ns/op
ok      ./chapter9/4_benchmarking    2.492s
```

On my 2013 Macbook Air, the benchmark runs half a million times and takes a little under 5,000 nanoseconds per run. Not bad at all!

Benchmark Regressions

One approach that I find useful is to add tests that expect benchmarks to perform at a certain speed. This enables me to have my test suite fail if the performance of a piece of code slows beyond a threshold I've set.

To do this, you can use the `testing.Benchmark` method, which takes a function with the same method signature as a benchmark function and returns a `testing.BenchmarkResult` type containing information about the benchmark. We can reuse the `BenchmarkRequestNewImageUnauthenticated` code here, and check that the benchmark isn't taking too long:

4_benchmarking/auth_test.go (excerpt)

```
// auth_test.go
func TestRequestNewImageUnauthenticatedPerformance(t *testing.T) {
    result := testing.Benchmark(func(b *testing.B) {
        request, _ := http.NewRequest("GET", "/images/new", nil)

        recorder := httptest.NewRecorder()
        app := NewApp()

        for i := 0; i < b.N; i++ {
            app.ServeHTTP(recorder, request)
        }
    })

    speed := result.NsPerOp()
    if speed > 4000 {
        t.Error("Expected response to take less than 4000
```

```
➡nanoseconds, but took", speed)
    }
}
```

We pass the benchmarking function to `testing.Benchmark` and then check the speed of the resulting run. In this case I've tested it against 4,000 nanoseconds, which I know is significantly slower than the benchmark runs, so I expect that this one will fail and tell me about it:

```
--- FAIL: TestRequestNewImageUnauthenticatedPerformance (2.52
➡seconds)
    auth_test.go:52: Expected response to take less than 4000
➡nanoseconds, but took 4927
FAIL
exit status 1
FAIL    ./chapter9/4_benchmarking   2.539s
```

So now we've created a test function that will actively warn us when the performance of our application starts to degrade. It's worth noting that this benchmark will run in all test runs, since it's a test function and not a benchmark function. The benchmark takes nearly three seconds to run, so it makes no sense to run this benchmark every time you're running your test suite. To get around this, you can run the test tool with the `-short` flag, and add a check to `testing.Short()` inside the benchmark. This will allow you to skip slow tests when you want to:

```
                              4_benchmarking/auth_test.go (excerpt)

func TestRequestNewImageUnauthenticatedPerformance(t *testing.T) {
    // Don't run the benchmark if we're doing short tests
    if testing.Short() {
        return
    }

    result := testing.Benchmark(func(b *testing.B) {
        request, _ := http.NewRequest("GET", "/images/new", nil)

        recorder := httptest.NewRecorder()
        app := NewApp()

        for i := 0; i < b.N; i++ {
            app.ServeHTTP(recorder, request)
        }
```

```
    })

    speed := result.NsPerOp()
    if speed > 4000 {
        t.Error("Expected response to take less than 4000
➥nanoseconds, but took", speed)
    }
}
```

And now by running go `test` `-short`, we'll see that everything is running to speed again:

```
PASS
ok      ./chapter9/4_benchmarking      0.016s
```

Summary

That's it for this chapter. We've covered how to write tests for various parts of Gophr, including testing HTTP requests both to and from the application, creating mock interfaces to test different method responses and avoid unnecessary work, and using functions stored in variables to swap out code when running tests. We've also looked at how we benchmark our code to ensure that it runs quickly, and add regression benchmarks to make sure our code stays fast as we continue to build our applications.

In the final chapter, we're going to have a look at how to make production-ready applications, including packaging our code into separate logical units, managing dependencies, and compiling code for other platforms.

Exercises

The NewUser tests we wrote using MockUserStore lack 100% code coverage for NewUser. Add error checking and any other validation required for full coverage of NewUser. For password and ID checking, you could either use the bcrypt.Compare-HashAndPassword method, or simply check that a string of a certain length has been generated.

Chapter **10**

Packaging and Production

In this last chapter we'll look at two distinct items. First, we're going to check out how you can make reusable packages to share between projects, or even modularize your code within a single project. Then we'll look at how to get your code into production, and the various methods for dependency management that the Go community uses.

Creating Packages

So far we've created all our code in the `main` package, and only consumed other packages. Eventually you're likely to want to split code that fits together as a logical module into its own package. Having code in a separate package means that you can encapsulate all the logic into a single area, as well as hide a lot of the internal workings from other packages, ensuring that your code is being used exactly as intended. In addition, writing code in packages can quite often influence how you design it in the first place, since only the types, variables, functions, and methods that you choose to export are available to the code that calls it.

What is a package?

Defining a **package** is easy: you just need to pick a name and place all your code in a directory of the same name. Instead of declaring `package main` at the top of each source file, make it the name of the package instead; for example, `package image`.

 Non-directory Package Names

You don't *have* to give the directory the same name as the package, but it is the convention and will serve you well as everything matches up that way. It makes it easier for a third party to hit the ground running with your code, too, since the package name matches the URL path, and is generally a lot more readable as the `import` statement matches the code usage. For example, if you create a package called "potato" and host it on Github, chances are that it will be imported as `github.com/your_username/potato`. Having a different package name to the path name would lead to some confusion; for example, a package "fries" at the same URL would confuse matters as you'd be unable to scan the code and immediately work out which import statement the package had come from.

All the files in a directory must belong to the same package, so avoid mixing names as this will result in a compile time error along the lines of `can't load package: found packages foo (foo.go) and bar (bar.go)`.

An Example Package

Let's create an example package, just to dip our toes in the water. We'll call it `foo`, and add a single function `PrintFoo` that prints out the string "foo":

examples/1_pkg_foo/foo/foo.go

```go
package foo

import "fmt"

func PrintFoo() {
    fmt.Println("foo")
}
```

Now we can call our `PrintFoo` function from a `main` package:

```
package main

import "./foo"

func main() {
    foo.PrintFoo()
}
```

You can run this code by running go run main.go inside the same directory as main.go, but if you try to run go build you'll see an error thrown. It's going to complain about local import '. /foo' in non-local package because it's expecting a fully qualified path relative to your $GOPATH. You can solve this by referencing this path to your library. If the code was in a directory $GOPATH/src/github.com/snikch/example, I'd need to update my import statement to import "github.com/snikch/example/foo", as that is the correct location of the package when Go tries to find it in the file system. It's no longer a local package relative to the current directory but a full import path relative to your $GOPATH. Try this now with your own example. It might take some time to get your head around it, but it's important to understand how to correctly set up your directory structure.

Exporting

I mentioned earlier that only exported functions, methods, and so on can be accessed from outside a package. This is a very simple concept, and is how you design your package API. If you start a function with an uppercase letter, it's exported. If you start it with a lowercase letter, it isn't. Only code inside a package can run code that isn't exported. This applies to functions, global variables and constants, types, and methods:

```
package foo

import "fmt"

type Bar struct {
    Visible bool
    hidden  bool
}
```

```
func NewBar() Bar {
    return Bar{
        Visible: true,
        hidden:  true,
    }
}

func (bar Bar) String() string {
    return bar.status()
}
func (bar Bar) status() string {
    return fmt.Sprintf("Visible is %T and hidden is %T",
➥bar.Visible, bar.hidden)
}
```

Here we have a package called `foo`. It contains an exported type `Bar` that we can access from outside the package, and a function `NewBar` that creates an instance of `Bar` for us. This type has two fields, one exported and one not, and two methods, one exported and one not.

You'll see that the exported method `String` is perfectly capable of calling the method `status`. Since it's in the same package, this is no problem. If you were to try to call `status` yourself from outside the package, you would attract an error such as: `myBar.status undefined (cannot refer to unexported field or method foo.Bar."".status)`. Likewise, you can't access the field `hidden`, but you can access `Visible`.

Generally speaking, only code that you want to actively encourage the package users to consume should be exported. If you're unsure whether or not to export a value, chances are you shouldn't. It's a lot easier to leave values unexported and then change them when you realise you need to access them, than export them and leave your packages open to being used in a way that wasn't quite how you intended.

Avoiding Circular Imports

Deciding how to structure your packages can be quite tricky, as the responsibilities of the various bits of code aren't always clear-cut. It's easy to end up with circular dependencies, with two packages trying to import each other. The circular dependency might not be caused by a direct import, it might be several imports deep; for instance, you might have package `a` that imports package `b` that imports package foo that then tries to import package a again. If you find yourself with these circular imports, you may need to rethink how your data is structured.

Interfaces are a good way to decouple packages, as you can implement an interface for a package without having to import the package. Since an interface is implicitly satisfied by simply implementing the required methods, no direct relationship with the package that defines the interface is necessary.

Let's Implement a Real Package

Some of the code we've written for the Gophr project in previous chapters is a perfect candidate for splitting out into its own package. The simplest example is the Middleware type. It provides a generic middleware interface that allows us to chain http.Handler types together, and is a very encapsulated piece of code—it has no dependencies except the net/http package that's part of the standard library.

To break this out into its own package, you first must decide where to put it. If could put it at the root of your $GOPATH/src directory, such as $GOPATH/src/middleware, and then import it as import "middleware". If you wanted to share or distribute your code, however, chances are you're likely to use a service such as Github, where you could create a new Git repository for the package and host it on Github's service. If you created a Git repository "middleware" on Github, you'd create the package on your system at $GOPATH/src/github.com/YOUR_GITHUB_USERNAME/middleware, and import it as import "github.com/YOUR_GITHUB_USERNAME/middleware".

Give that a try now. Move the file **middleware.go** from your Gophr project into its own folder inside your $GOPATH. Then update its first line to read package middleware, so that it knows it's no longer in the main package. Now update your main application to correctly import and call the middleware package, since it's expected it to be in the same package so far. This is done in the file main.go, where you should replace the two instances where Middleware is referenced with middleware.Middleware in func NewApp(). Here's what the NewApp function should look like after the update:

1_pkg_web/main.go *(excerpt)*

```
func NewApp() middleware.Middleware {
    router := NewRouter()
```

```
router.Handle("GET", "/", HandleHome)
router.Handle("GET", "/register", HandleUserNew)
router.Handle("POST", "/register", HandleUserCreate)
router.Handle("GET", "/login", HandleSessionNew)
router.Handle("POST", "/login", HandleSessionCreate)
router.Handle("GET", "/image/:imageID", HandleImageShow)
router.Handle("GET", "/user/:userID", HandleUserShow)

router.ServeFiles(
    "/assets/*filepath",
    http.Dir("assets/"),
)
router.ServeFiles(
    "/im/*filepath",
    http.Dir("data/images/"),
)

secureRouter := NewRouter()
secureRouter.Handle("GET", "/sign-out", HandleSessionDestroy)
secureRouter.Handle("GET", "/account", HandleUserEdit)
secureRouter.Handle("POST", "/account", HandleUserUpdate)
secureRouter.Handle("GET", "/images/new", HandleImageNew)
secureRouter.Handle("POST", "/images/new", HandleImageCreate)

middleware := middleware.Middleware{}
middleware.Add(router)
middleware.Add(http.HandlerFunc(RequireLogin))
middleware.Add(secureRouter)

return middleware
}
```

Package Exercise

As an exercise, try finding some areas of the Gophr code that are nice and encapsulated, and split them out into their own package. An example of this might be your database access and configuration, another good example is the entire user system, including the types, handlers and templates. There are no right or wrong answers here, and you may find that once you try splitting code out it's not as cut and dried as you expected—but there's no better way to understand how this works than by rolling up your sleeves and doing it yourself.

Dependency Management

Gone are the days where you download a zip file of a individual's code, place its contents in a folder in your project somewhere, start using it, and never think about it again. Dependency management is all about managing the third-party packages you use. At its core, it's about making your software easy to install, update, and compile. While this might sound simple enough to solve, it's often complicated by various factors such as conflicting versions and network availability. If both your code and a third-party package you utilize employ different versions of another third-party package—how do you handle that?

Go's built-in dependency management makes it very easy to be up and running with a package, but without providing a great suite for production-level control. The `go get` tool we've already seen is good for getting a package from source control—somewhere on the Internet—onto your machine so that you can immediately start using it. The `-u` flag allows you to update the package, but there's no fine-grained control over what you're downloading; you're just downloading the latest version of the code on the master branch.

 Master Branch Defined

In these examples, I'm referring to the "master branch" as that is what it's called in Git. What I really mean is the latest revision of the code. Some source control systems call it the "tip," "main," or "trunk."

That might sound okay at first, but let's play out a scenario. You're working in a team of two along with Sarah, another Go developer. You decide to use a third-party package that lets you query an Elasticsearch[1] cluster. You write your code, and it's compiling and working well! You commit your code, push it up to your source control, and ask Sarah to do a code review. She pulls down your code, runs `go get .`, and has the dependencies installed for her including the Elasticsearch package. Sounds great, right?

Except what if the owner of the Elasticsearch package has changed how the package works? What if they've rewritten the code so that instead of global query functions, you have to manually create a connection and query it? All of a sudden your

---

[1] http://en.wikipedia.org/wiki/Elasticsearch

code—which was working fine—is failing to compile and errors are flowing everywhere. Sarah is trying to use completely different code to what you were using.

This isn't hypothetical; this is a real-life situation that occurred to me in my early days as a Go developer. While the community has an unwritten rule of trying to avoid breaking changes to the master branch of a package, it's inevitable that breaking changes have to be made. If you want to avoid being stung by a user's changes breaking your code, you'll need a way to manage these dependencies.

What can you do? How do you ensure that everyone is receiving the same versions of the code? There's no definitive answer to this question from the Go authors, and up until this point they've let the community create its own tools to solve this problem. So I'm going to discuss two methods of managing packages: one as an end user, and another as a package maintainer, so that your users can safely utilize your package.

 Watch This Space

At the time of writing, the Go authors are seeking community feedback on a better dependency management system. While this will eventually solve the problems of dependency versions, it won't be available in the near term. I look forward to sections of this chapter becoming irrelevant, though!

Godep

Godep is a tool written in Go that allows you to copy your dependency code directly into your source control and then restore it back into your `$GOPATH`. The process of saving third-party dependencies such as this is often called **vendoring**.

To install the `godep` command, run `go get github.com/tools/godep`. This will install Godep and make it available to you in your command line. We'll use the Gophr project from previous chapters, and use Godep to save the dependencies.

 Custom Packages

If you've followed along with the custom package examples earlier in this chapter, you may have made a new package yet to be in source control. This could break Godep, since it expects all packages to be in source control. If you run into errors along the lines of "xyx is not using a known version control system," grab a new copy of the Gophr project from the code archive for this book.

Saving Your Dependencies

To vendor all your dependencies, run `godep save` inside the project directory. A log stream of all the files being copied will be shown, and once complete you'll see that a new **Godeps** directory has been created as evident in Figure 10.1.

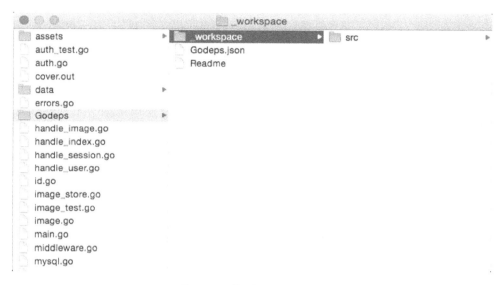

Figure 10.1. The Godeps directory

The Godeps folder contains three items, the first of which, a **Readme** file, contains little information except for a link to the Godep website. What's important are the **Godeps.json** file, which describes all the dependencies and their source control version information, and the **_workspace** directory, shown in Figure 10.2, which contains a complete copy of the dependencies and is set up like your $GOPATH:

```
                                           2_godeps/Godeps/Godeps.json

// Godeps/Godeps.json
{
    "ImportPath": "github.com/spbooks/go1/chapter10/2_godeps",
    "GoVersion": "go1.4",
    "Deps": [
        {
            "ImportPath": "code.google.com/p/go.crypto/bcrypt",
```

```
                    "Comment": "null-219",
                    "Rev": "00a7d3b31bbab5795b4a51933c04fc2768242970"
        },
        {

                    "ImportPath": "code.google.com/p/go.crypto/blowfish",
                    "Comment": "null-219",
                    "Rev": "00a7d3b31bbab5795b4a51933c04fc2768242970"
        },
        {

                    "ImportPath": "github.com/disintegration/imaging",
                    "Rev": "4685da8f7d9ed48a7d6b8982fd966d4fd83b4d2e"
        },
        {

                    "ImportPath": "github.com/go-sql-driver/mysql",
                    "Comment": "v1.2-1-g7094cf0",
                    "Rev": "7094cf0331ed6bde3cd75aa5d1da0e7764b526c9"
        },
        {

                    "ImportPath": "github.com/julienschmidt/httprouter",
                    "Rev": "afa7ae29ca847252b56d9279b6a012c1a7a5e225"
        },
        {

                    "ImportPath": "golang.org/x/image/bmp",
                    "Rev": "0351284b2d72e390b79229a0c9fe426b3d8db78d"
        },
        {

                    "ImportPath": "golang.org/x/image/tiff",
                    "Rev": "0351284b2d72e390b79229a0c9fe426b3d8db78d"
```

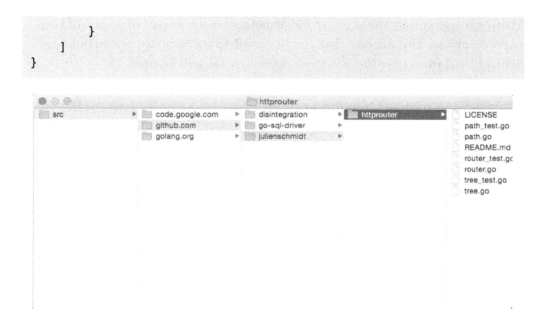

Figure 10.2. The Godeps workspace

The entire **godeps** folder should be committed to source control. Yes—that means you've duplicated all the code and added to the size of your project, but now you have the ability to rebuild your project in the exact state it was in when you ran **godep save**. This shouldn't be underestimated, as it means that the sites hosting the packages can go down and you can build and deploy your code from a new machine that's never seen your project before.

Using Dependencies

Once vendored into **Godeps/_workspace**, you have two options for using these files. You can either run commands through the **godep** command, which will run the **go** tool with a custom $GOPATH set up to provide access to the vendored dependencies, or you can run **godep restore** to update all the dependencies in your $GOPATH with the versions from the **_workspace** directory.

Generally, the best process is for developers to always run **godep restore** to ensure that their dependencies are up to date; then they can continue to use the standard Go tools without having to use the **godep** tool at all. This simple process won't affect your workflow much at all.

There are appropriate times to use the `godep` tool, such as part of your build and deploy process. This ensures that you're unable to accidentally use an outdated dependency, since only the vendored dependencies will be used.

Saving without Vendoring

Godep also provides the ability to create your `Godeps.json` file without copying the source files into the directory. Running `godep restore` will use the version information in `Godeps/Godeps.json` to attempt to check out the correct versions inside your `$GOPATH`. While this might seem a more straightforward solution—since Godep can then check out the exact versions required without copying the source—it still leaves your ability to build your project at the whim of external source control providers, and I wouldn't recommend it.

Multiple Packages

If your project contains many packages rather than a single buildable one, it's unnecessary to run `godep save` inside each package and have multiple `Godeps` directories. Instead, you can run `godep save ./...` from the parent directory and it will vendor all the subpackage dependencies into a single `Godeps` directory. Alternatively, you can run `godep restore ./...` to restore all the subpackage dependencies.

The gopkg.in Service

Unfortunately, Godep is less helpful when you're writing a package to be used by other code. To work around this, there are several services that allow you to create an import URL to point to a specific version of your code. With these systems you make a promise, as the package author, that you won't make breaking changes to the API of your package within a specific version. A **version** is usually defined as a specific branch, or tag, in your source control.

A popular instance of this style of dependency management that works with Github repos is the service gopkg.in.[2] Instead of importing directly from Github, you import a gopkg.in URL that maps to a Github repo on a specific branch. For example, if you were to import `gopkg.in/your_username/potato.v3`, that would effectively be importing the branch v3 of your repository at `github.com/your_username/potato`.

---

[2] http://labix.org/gopkg.in

The gopkg.in URL actually provides a gateway Git repository to do this, which is pretty cool.

If no matching version is available, you'll see an error. Every Github repo has a v0 version that maps to the master branch, but this falls short of providing much in the way of security; however, you can supply this URL to your package users as a way of saying that the package is in beta or alpha mode, indicating that you're unable to promise a stable API at present, but they should check back for when one might be available.

So instead of having your **Readme** file advising to install via Github, you should document your package as being available at its gopkg.in URL. Now the users of your package will be locked in to the version that they've chosen, and you've promised not to make any breaking changes to that version. This moves the decision to update away from the package maintainer to the owner of the consuming code, reducing the chance of bugs being introduced through dependencies.

Deploying Go Applications

Once your application is complete and you're ready to run it on a server, you have two options: you can either compile it on the server, or compile it on your machine and send it to the server. Both methods have their pros and cons.

A Go binary is a completely encapsulated, executable file. This means that it doesn't need to call out to other libraries external to the binary itself. It's one of the reasons why Go is loved by sysadmins, as they know that once a binary is on the server, there will be no dependency issues or requirement to install other pieces of software.

Compiling on the Server

Compiling on the server is often one of the fastest ways to get your updated code built and running. You can just pull down the latest code, ensure that your dependencies are up to date, and compile your binary—ready to go. This might look a little like this:

```
cd MY_PROJECT_DIR/
git pull
godep restore
go build
./my_project # run the project binary
```

The downside to this process is that you must have all the software required to build your project on the server. Do you have Git on your server, so you can download the project code? Do you even have Go installed? While it's generally faster to download and compile on the machine, the initial setup is an overhead that you might want to avoid.

Compiling Elsewhere

Another method is to compile the binary on another machine, such as your development machine, and copy it to your server. This way it's unnecessary for your server to have Git or even Go installed. This might sound a bit odd at first, as it's not really common practice. What if you're running Mac OS on your computer and your server is Linux? How could that possibly work?

Well, what's great is that you can do this! Go has the ability to **cross-compile** for different platforms, so you can compile for Linux directly on your Mac OS or Windows machine. As mentioned earlier, the entire program is a single executable with no external dependencies once compiled, and this is the key to being able to cross-compile.

Before continuing, I should note that cross-compilation can become a little hairy for people who are unused to compiling software from source. It requires access to a C compiler, and for some platforms can be quite complicated.

Cross-compiling

 Go Compiling Go

At the time of writing, Go 1.4 is the current release, and setting up cross-compilation requires a bit of work. The reasons for this are twofold: firstly, the Go compiler is written in C and requires a platform-specific compiler to be able to compile for a different platform. Secondly, a standard library for the target platform is required. The compiler that ships with Go 1.5, however, is written in Go itself. Because of this, cross-platform standard library code is included as part of the release, and the compiler works cross-platform (it's Go!), meaning that cross-compilation comes for free with no setup needed.

The first item required for cross-compiling is access to the Go source code. If you compiled your Go installation from source, this step is redundant. The Go team have instructions for this,[3] and if you already have `gcc` (a C compiler) installed, it should be as simple as this:

```
git clone https://go.googlesource.com/go
cd go/src
git checkout go1.4.1
./all.bash
```

If all goes successfully, you'll see this final output:

```
ALL TESTS PASSED

---

Installed Go for darwin/amd64 in /Users/mal/Go-install-test/go
Installed commands in /Users/mal/Go-install-test/go/bin
*** You need to add /Users/mal/Go-install-test/go/bin to your PATH.
```

The `all.bash` script is responsible for building Go from source and running the full test suite, which is why we see the "ALL TESTS PASSED" message.

 Windows Users

Windows users will need to run the `.bat` version of all `.bash` commands in this chapter; for example, `./make.bash` becomes **make.bat**. The scripts all perform the same way, they're just specific to the platform. Linux and Mac OS users will be able to run the `.bash` files.

Once you've compiled Go, you'll have to update your system to use this Go installation rather than any previous one. Remove any existing Go `bin` directory from your PATH, and add the new `bin` directory from your freshly compiled install. The final task is to make sure the environment variable `GOROOT` is set to the directory into which you cloned the Go source code. On my Windows system this was **C:\Gosrc**.

---

[3] https://golang.org/doc/install/source

Note that there is a directory **src** inside the GOROOT; do not include that directory when setting your GOROOT.

 Getting a C Compiler

If you don't have **gcc** installed, you'll need to get your hands on it for your system. To establish whether you already have it installed, run **gcc** in your command line. If you receive an error stating that the program can't be found, you don't have it.

For **gcc** on Windows, install TDM-GCC,[4] on Mac OS install Xcode[5] and the command line tools, and on Linux use your package manager.

The most up-to-date information about installing will always be on the Go website.[6]

Building Go for Other Platforms

Before you can build binaries for other platforms, you'll have to build Go itself for those platforms, but you need only do this once for each platform you'd like to target. First, specify both the operating system and architecture via the environment variables GOOS and GOARCH. You can easily supply environment variables when running a command by prefixing the command with key-value pairs like so: VARI-ABLE_NAME=variable_value. If the variables are unavailable, the build scripts use the host OS and architecture, which is why building Go usually creates a working install for your system.

Most of the time, you'll be compiling for darwin (Mac OS 10.6+), linux, or windows as the operating system, and either amd64 or 386 as the architecture choice for 64-bit or 32-bit respectively. Most systems these days are 64-bit, but older machines may be 32-bit. Go also compiles for the arm architecture if you're doing embedded device work. There are a variety of other combinations that I won't include here, but an up-to-date list is always available on the Go website.[7]

Compiling for another platform with **all.bash** will most likely give you some failure errors, as some tests being platform-specific will be unable to run. This shouldn't

---

[4] http://tdm-gcc.tdragon.net/

[5] https://developer.apple.com/xcode/

[6] https://golang.org/doc/install/source

[7] https://golang.org/doc/install/source

pose a problem as the stable Go releases should have a fully passing test suite. Instead of using `all.bash` we'll use `make.bash`, which is usually invoked as part of the larger build process. This will simply compile Go for the target OS and architecture, and install to the **$GOROOT/src/pkg** directory. Go ahead now and compile for another platform. If you're on Windows, you might like to compile for Linux, and vice versa.

Mac OS and Linux

Here's how to build Go for Mac OS and Linux:

```
GOOS=linux GOARCH=amd64 ./make.bash
```

```
Installed Go for linux/amd64 in /Users/mal/Go-install-test/go
Installed commands in /Users/mal/Go-install-test/go/bin
GOOS=linux GOARCH=amd64 ./make.bash  43.35s user 10.00s system 234%
➥cpu 22.733 total
```

Once run, you'll see a similar message to that shown in the previous section, but without the "ALL TESTS PASSED" message. At this point, you'll be able to build a project binary for the target platform. You can view the platforms available by looking in the **$GOROOT/pkg** directory:

```
ls -l $GOROOT/pkg
total 0
drwxr-xr-x  58 mal  admin  1972 May 10 08:02 darwin_amd64
drwxr-xr-x  58 mal  admin  1972 May 10 08:08 linux_amd64
drwxr-xr-x   7 mal  admin   238 Aug 20  2014 obj
drwxr-xr-x   4 mal  admin   136 Aug 20  2014 tool
```

Here we have Go compiled for 64-bit versions of both Linux and Mac OS (darwin).

Windows

You'll need to set the GOOS and GOARCH environment variables before running **make.bat**. This will set them for the entire terminal session; so if you reopen your shell, you'll have to set them again:

```
set GOOS=linux
set GOARCH=amd64
make.bat
```

```
---
Installed Go for linux/amd64 in C:\Gosrc
Installed commands in C:\Gosrc\bin
```

Here we've compiled Go for Linux. At this point we're able to build a project binary for the target platform. We can view the platforms available by looking in the **%GOROOT%\pkg** directory:

```
C:\Gosrc\src>dir %GOROOT\pkg
 Directory of C:\Gosrc\pkg

03/13/2015  01:14 PM    <DIR>          .
03/13/2015  01:14 PM    <DIR>          ..
03/13/2015  01:15 PM    <DIR>          linux_amd64
03/13/2015  01:14 PM    <DIR>          obj
03/13/2015  01:15 PM    <DIR>          tool
03/13/2015  01:15 PM    <DIR>          windows_amd64
               0 File(s)              0 bytes
               7 Dir(s)  177,102,487,552 bytes free
```

Here you can see we have both Windows and Linux 64-bit installs of Go.

Building Binaries for Other Platforms

Once we have Go built for a platform, we can build our projects for that platform as well. The process is similar—we just run the go build command with the GOOS and GOARCH environment variables like we did when we compiled Go. We can see this in action by compiling the Gophr project for another platform.

On Mac OS or Linux:

```
GOOS=linux GOARCH=amd64 go build -o gophr_linux_amd64
```

On Windows:

```
set GOOS=linux
set GOARCH=amd64
go build -o gophr_linux_amd64
```

You'll see that I've set the flag -o to gophr_linux_amd64. The -o flag lets you set an output file for the binary. Since we're compiling for another platform, it's best to specify a platform-specific binary name. We'll now have a file gophr_linux_amd64 that you can upload to a 64-bit Linux system and run without any other dependencies. Here I'm referring to system dependencies to actually run the compiled binary. Since the Gophr project serves up files such as our templates and CSS, these will also need to be uploaded to any system you run the binary on.

 Accessing a Linux Server

There are a variety of ways to test out cross-compiling to a Linux server. (This is assuming you're not running Linux as your main operating system, in which case you probably know how to access a Windows or Mac OS system.) You can download and run a "Live CD" of Ubuntu Linux[8] on your own computer or in a virtual machine using software such as VirtualBox. A Live CD is the regular installer, but it enables you to run the operating system without having to install it permanently to disk. You can also spin up a box in the cloud using a cloud server provider such as Amazon EC2, Digital Ocean, or Microsoft Azure. Most cloud server providers offer a generous free tier to get started with.

That's All, Folks!

In this chapter, we've had a look at how to create packages for code reuse and the encapsulation of logic. We also looked at some of the real-world issues of sharing code and managing dependencies, both for the programs you write and the packages you intend to share. Lastly we learned how we can build our programs for a completely different architecture and operating system—all from the comfort of our own computers. This can be quite a lot to take in, but it's the everyday bread and butter of a Go developer, and well worth learning.

That brings us to the end of our journey together with Go; however, I hope it's just the start of *your* journey with Go. By now you should have a good understanding of how Go works, why developers are flocking to it for its ease of use and portability,

---

[8] http://www.ubuntu.com/download/desktop

and why you might want to use it for your next project. I look forward to seeing you become a part of the Go community!

www.ingramcontent.com/pod-product-compliance
Lightning Source LLC
Chambersburg PA
CBHW080400060326
40689CB00019B/4085